The Soil & Soul Connection

**Written by
Charlie Cole**

**Illustrated by
Lisa Smith**

ISBN: 1-4107-2329-1 (e-book)
ISBN: 1-4107-2330-5 (Paperback)
ISBN: 1-4107-4278-4 (Dust Jacket)

Library of Congress Control Number: 2003091089

This book is printed on acid free paper.

Printed in the United States of America
Bloomington, IN

1stBooks - rev. 04/14/03

To Our Readers—

We want to thank you for the privilege to come into your life and share a few moments. Our hope is that we might have offered a few pictures or words that will help make your adventure of life more enjoyable. We believe that this world was created with beauty and precision and solely intended for our use and enjoyment. Our hope is that in some small and simple way, our insights and ideas will add a little extra peace, happiness, and serenity to this earthly journey of your soul.

Charlie & Lisa

Contents

An Introduction

A hundred years ago, most people in America lived on farms or in small towns. The farms were small by today's standards and were tended by a family. These farms were to a great extent self-sufficient. They had hogs, cattle, and chickens for meat, milk, and eggs, a garden and some fruit trees. They raised hay and grain to feed the livestock and planned for some surplus of grain or produce to buy the things they couldn't grow and to pay the taxes and mortgage. Horses, strong backs, and good neighbors powered these farms. The farm was more than a commercial venture; it was a lifestyle closely connected to the good earth.

The towns were the centers of trade for the surrounding area. They provided the things that could not be grown on the farm and provided a market for the surpluses raised on the farm. Other than the rural one-room schools, they were the centers for education and they were the social center for the surrounding area. The town and farms were mutually dependent on each other and they also shared a close connection to the good earth. This was rural America and the values that were basic to these farms and towns were what made America great.

Rural America inspired the "American Dream". That dream included independence, freedom, and opportunity. It included a certain peace, serenity and satisfaction that came as a reward for honest effort. Contrary to today's concept of that dream, it was of middle class proportions. It did not include continuous expansion, but rather of a farm that a family could manage, pay off a mortgage, and have a little to help the next generation. The merchants in those small towns did not dream of supermarkets and malls, but rather a business that would support a comfortable home and lifestyle. Both were content with comfort and security rather than great wealth and luxury.

Early rural America had a good work ethic. Most work was physically demanding and entailed a great deal of craftsmanship and society expected everyone to earn his keep. A certain amount of pride was the result of these expectations and laziness and poor workmanship were not acceptable.

A good work ethic included honesty and integrity and in a small close knit community, a good reputation was very important.

Rural America fostered strong family values. The whole family was needed to run the farm or business. These families worked together, ate together, and played together. As children, there were chores to do and responsibilities to be met. Meals required a great deal of preparation, so everyone ate at the same time. What today we label as entertainment was very scarce, so they played together in a spontaneous and unstructured way. There was the porch swing for summer evenings, board games and books for long winter evenings, and picnics for holidays. A strong family was almost necessary. Husbands needed good wives to maintain a good home. Wives needed good husbands to provide the physical strength needed on the farm or business. Children needed both parents to provide proper guidance and the necessities of life, because there were no institutions to do so, except as a last resort.

Rural America was religious. Much education was based on the Scriptures, Bibles were in almost every home and weddings and funerals were of a religious nature. In many cases, the church was the social center of a community and Sunday was regarded as a day of rest, worship, and family fun.

The influence of rural America was felt in the cities. Many in the cities had family roots in the country because parents, grandparents, or aunts and uncles still lived on a farm. Because of the great numbers in rural America, it was even a powerful political bloc. The industries and commerce in the cities coveted the work ethic, which was a way of life on the farm. The rich soil and favorable climate of America allowed the farms to produce an abundance of food at a reasonable price, which allowed the middle class money available for a comfortable lifestyle.

Please understand that this description of rural America is prejudiced toward the positive. There were bad times down on the farm. There were times of bad weather and low prices. There was sickness, pain, injustice, sorrow, and death. Life, wherever it may be, includes all of these and, cruel as it may seem, such things are even necessary to form strong character. Bad times were a part of rural America but overcoming such obstacles only made it stronger.

The value of any victory is determined by the strength of the opposition.

Sadly, we have lost much of our rural heritage. The ancestor on the farm is more often several generations removed. Even farms are specialized to the point they lack any resemblance to self-sufficiency. Transportation and communication has closely connected rural life to urban life and the "American Dream" has changed from independence, freedom, and comfort to ease, wealth, and luxury. We have lost our connection to the soil; even by many whom make their livelihood from the good earth. For these changes we suffer. Hopefully, the next few thoughts and experiences will be helpful in connecting us once again our very soul to our precious soil.

Dirt

I am a simple dirt farmer and because of this vocation, I get my hands dirty. By dirty hands, I mean some of the good earth gets on my hands and even under my fingernails. I want to protest the modern conception that accumulating this dirt is an unclean or unsanitary condition. It washes off easily and has no ill effects. The accumulation that might show on my hands is a small portion of the very essence of life. According to the Scriptures, mankind was formed from the dust of the earth and by all logic his body will return to the good earth. In the meantime, the products of that good earth will nourish him. His health and well being are totally and directly dependent on what is so inappropriately called "dirt". Dirt, soil and filth seem to be used interchangeably, when in reality, any reference to the good earth should be one of the utmost respect. This good earth, on which we are so dependent, is in reality a complicated Eco-system and to us who till it and love it, a priceless heritage of which we are only stewards for a brief time.

Because of mechanization and technology, and even in some cases, the inappropriate and misplaced association of the good earth and filth, many people seem to distance themselves from this so-called dirt. Even many of those who earn their livelihood from the soil, often do so at a distance with a steering wheel, rubber tires, and even in some cases gloves to keep themselves from actual contact with the soil. While machinery is necessary to produce the quantity of food necessary to feed the world, some "hands on" contact seems only appropriate.

While it may not be actual "hands on" contact, over the years, I have spent many hours using a hoe or a shovel and usually these hours have not been the most enjoyable. Using these tools is physically demanding, the weather may not be ideal, and often the use of these tools indicate that some weeds are growing or that some drain is not functioning properly. Such contact with the good earth, even though the circumstances are less than favorable, provide some very good exercise, and can stimulate some very constructive thinking. I would like to share some "corn field philosophy" that sometimes develops while in such contact with the good earth, or to some, dirt.

Our old world is a troubled place. It has always has been plagued by wars, pestilence, and famine, and man's cruelty to man is evident in many places and occurs often. As the world gets more crowded and systems of communication can connect us to any spot on the earth in an instant, we are more aware of these problems whether they be far away or close to home. Our technology has invaded our privacy to the point that by just punching a few buttons, anyone can find many things about me that once were regarded as personal. As I read the newspapers, I become aware that many streets in most large cities could pose a physical danger to me even if my business was honorable. I read the statistics on broken families, abuse, single parents, and un-wed mothers and can only conclude that the institution of the family is at risk. I remember a carefree childhood and happy teen years when drugs and shootings were unheard of and suicide was something old people did when they couldn't pay their bills or the law was closing in. As I observe my younger friends and acquaintances, they shed far more tears than those I knew at a comparable age. Society does seem to recognize these problems, at least they talk about them, but only offer political solutions, fund expensive studies, or organize support groups. Any of these solutions can cure a hurt not prevent it. From a very early age, our society encourages and educates us to run at a fast pace with the lure of fame and fortune as the highest goals in life, and then, so often, after much time and effort, many discover that something is still missing and that neither fame or fortune is the key to happiness. As I view the news, I am concerned about the way we allow differences to separate us because we do not appreciate how unique we are as individuals. I believe that much of the wisdom that was acquired by maturity and experience has been discounted by a generation that ignores the heritage that makes their lifestyle possible, and believes that there will always be a tomorrow and they have little responsibility to make any tomorrow better. I meet so many people who fail to see beauty because they don't look for it, think they are not loved, but make little effort to be loveable, and don't enjoy the simple things because they make their lives to complicated. So many people seem to demand comfort and convenience and regard them as their rights rather than properly appreciating them. They command an arsenal of labor saving devices and only find themselves too busy to enjoy any time saved.

I can remember when it was not quite this way. I can remember a time when we had no telephone, electricity, or central heat. I can remember when we had to have a garden if we wanted to eat and all our meals were prepared from a "scratch". I also remember the cold and smelly outhouse, and the difficulty of reading by the light of a kerosene lamp. I would hate to return to those "good old days", and I would go to great lengths to keep my modern conveniences. But in spite of the poverty and inconvenience of those times, people I knew seemed to be just as happy as the people around me today. We knew our neighbors exchanged work with them, and knew that we could depend on them for help if needed. My parents were not professional musicians, but mom would softly sing as she worked and my dad would whistle as he went about his chores. We had a neighbor that could be heard singing from a great distance as he worked his fields. Families worked hard, played together, and ate together and doors were seldom locked at night. Today, most of these blessings seem to be lost.

Of course, it isn't scientific, but it seems quite a coincidence that all this change came at the same time we quit getting our hands "dirty". It seems very strange that a creature that could contrive all our conveniences couldn't retain or even enhance some of those past values and still have comfortable bathrooms and electric lights.

Historically, this has been a problem for mankind ever since he has recorded his adventures. History is crowded with stories of individuals and even nations that were greater while struggling than while basking in wealth and affluence and in so many cases, it was the wealth and affluence for which they expended so much effort that was their downfall. Ease, comfort, and the satisfaction of physical appetites are usually honorable lifetime goals for mankind, either as individual goals, or goals as reflected by society, and effort expended for such goals should be rewarded. But all too often, the effort expended for such goals is at the expense of other more worthwhile accomplishments. Families, close friendships, neighbors in need, and even personal happiness is often sacrificed in the name of "success". This is not to imply that we should not strive to better ourselves, but rather that we must learn how to handle "success".

Handling success does not come without effort and is not the course of least resistance. Too often, we forget those who helped along the way, too often, we misuse the power that success seems to bestow, too often, we get lazy and complacent, too often, we get greedy, too often, we worship the god of materialism instead of greater values, and too often, we over value our self-worth.

Digging dirt is often regarded as a humiliating endeavor, and it could be, but maybe humility is an overlooked virtue. Such a virtue is not a matter of esteem, but rather a matter of honest evaluation of who we really are, where we are headed, and a greater appreciation of the wonderful adventure we call life. A smear of the good earth on our Sunday clothes is appropriately called dirt, but it is the same good earth that grows the food for our nourishment, and even flowers for our enjoyment. It is important that we understand both situations.

K.I.S.S.

In our modern culture, there is a tendency to make everything complicated. It is true that our modern technology has made all of the mechanical wonders we watch, drive, or use in our daily lives very complicated and in so doing has made them more durable and useful, but has also made them harder, if not impossible, to repair. In almost every other walk of life, studies are made and fancy terminology devised to explain some wonderful idea or new process. A little reminder such as this may be in order. KISS means, "Keep It Simple Stupid" and it is very good advice. At times, life can become more meaningful, understandable, and manageable when we can reduce it to more simple terms. This is contrary to most modern thought and technology, but somehow, the more complicated we make life, the more problems we seem to have and the more complicated the solutions to these problems become.

Every year, I plant seeds, the seeds sprout and grow and produce more seeds of like kind. I know that a seed has one purpose for its existence, and that is to reproduce. One seed is usually capable of producing vast amounts of like kind and we take advantage of this trait to produce food and fiber for our consumption. The seed that I plant is capable of extracting the necessary nutrients for its growth and development from the soil, as long as they are available in that soil. The seed can flourish when the soil is tillable, has a proper amount of moisture available, adequate sunlight, and there is not too much competition from other plants. This is the simple basis of all agriculture. A seed is planted. The genetic make-up of the seed, the good earth, the rain, and the sun will cause a plant to grow. That plant can be utilized to sustain the life of its kind and produce enough seed for a harvest and some extra to start another generation.

This is a marvelous process. It produced food for wildlife and primitive man for countless generations with no human intervention. It is common knowledge that such a process worked long before anyone questioned how or why or even cultivated it in any way. Then this natural process started to get complicated. As population became denser and a desire to provide a more dependable supply emerged, it became necessary to produce more food and fiber on less land. Man, being the intelligent creature that he is, learned to increase yields through cultivation, selective breeding, then by hybridization, and now by even altering the genetic make-up of the plant itself. He has studied the growth process and has learned much, except how to duplicate the factor that causes life itself.

Man has also studied the soil and has learned that it too is a very complicated creation. We can test the soil and add necessary nutrients, provide the proper amount of water, and improve the texture, but a complete knowledge of how a plant takes energy from the sun and the nutrients from the good earth still remains an unlocked mystery.

This simple lesson learned from the soil is also pertinent to our lives. Our existence on earth is really very simple, but as with the seeds, we complicate it. We come into this world helpless and completely dependent on the nurture and love of parents. Physically, we take nutrients from the soil and grow and mature and we have the inherent capacity to explore, dare, and learn. We are blessed with senses that can make our existence pleasurable, unlike other creatures, which only exist to produce another generation, and assume their place on the food chain. Our Creator has endowed us with the ability to love and this gives our association with others the potential of being worth while and enjoyable. Our life span is relatively short and we will become frail, weak, and dependent on others, and eventually, our bodies will return to the soil that nurtured us. As with the seed, there is a portion of each of us which remains a mystery that the wisdom of the ages concludes will live eternally. We call it the soul.

If we could reduce life to its simplest form, our existence should be one of growth, happiness, serenity and pleasure, but as with the seed, there are things that complicate life. There are natural things, we must protect ourselves from adverse weather, assure ourselves of food and water, and defend ourselves from many kinds of danger. Nurturing the next generation adds complications to life. In too many cases, the next generation is regarded as a toy or a nuisance instead of a pleasure and an investment in our own future and the connecting link between generations. Instead of the most possible enjoyment of our senses, we allow our senses to be out master rather than our servant and we steer our ability to love into the wrong channels instead of sharing this sacred emotion with others. We chase material things, fame, and power and then, all too late, find we have missed the finer things in life. We forget our heritage and that we are the connecting link between generations and pass this sacred responsibility to governments and institutions. We take pride in our discoveries and forget to hold in awe the creation of things we discover and are prone to use our discoveries in a harmful manner.

We do live in a complicated world and that we cannot change. For a time, we might find an escape, but the world gets smaller and smaller and it gets harder and harder to find a more simple existence. The alternative is to look for the simple things and reduce complicated things to more simple dimensions. We might not be able to isolate ourselves in some deep dark forest, but we can appreciate and admire the trees in our own back yard. We do not have to be an astronomer to see the stars or a biologist to see the beauty of a flower. We do not need a degree in sociology to enjoy those around us or to help someone in need.

Life can indeed get complicated, the real enjoyment in living is in simplifying it rather than adding to the complications. Most of the problems we face are of our own making or our own attitudes because we fail to understand that everything we do has consequences. No deed is an act unto itself. We reap benefits or suffer consequences depending on what we sow, and somehow we find it hard to understand this simple rule of life. Understanding and practicing this simple rule of life is the first step in keeping life simple. Often, simple and important lessons in life are made complicated. Surveys, studies and reports are usually long and tedious and written with words of many syllables and in great detail to make some point, rather than common and ordinary experiences used as teachers of valuable lessons. K.I.S.S. is of great value in learning how to live a happy, serene, and productive life.

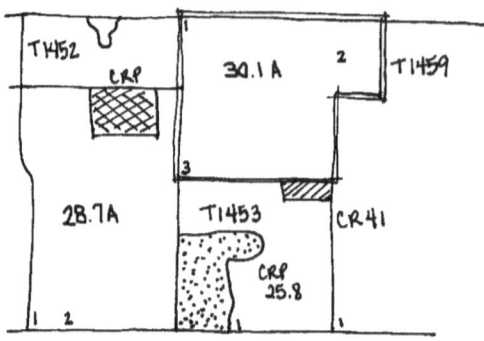

An Acre

My land is measured in acres. Maps are made, lines are drawn, and these are recorded by governments to assure ownership of land and for purposes of taxation. A map is a plane surface and two dimensional, but as a steward of the soil, I know that land has depth and is really three-dimensional. I am familiar with the terms topsoil and subsoil and the importance of each. I must plant seeds at a proper depth, I cannot just throw them on the top of the ground, and they must be in some way covered with the good earth to assure moisture. These seeds will send roots into the soil, so I also must be aware of the fertility that lies beneath the surface and do all I can to increase it or at least maintain it.

Far too many people seem to not understand this. Nations fight over land only as it appears on maps, industry covets land for places to erect factories, developers see land as an area to divide into saleable lots, commerce demands portions for roads and rails, and others see land as only spots for recreation. Only a few seem to understand the importance of the third dimension of the good earth.

Just as many are prone to regard the good earth as two dimensional, all too often many regard their lives as only two dimensional and overlook the fact they are not just photographs, but creatures with thoughts, ideas, emotions, and deeper values. This is not the familiar sermon on judgement of others, but rather a challenge to put more value on our own personal third dimension. People seem obsessed with their good looks. We adorn our bodies with fancy clothing, jewelry, and cosmetics and even regard physical fitness an attraction rather than a necessity for good health. Fortunes are spent on maintaining personal appearance and countless hours of precious time used to make ourselves as attractive as we possibly can. To a point, this is good. Being well groomed sends a message that we covet the respect of those around us. People like others to be well groomed and judge their desire to fit into society by their appearance. Our appearance does matter, but an equal amount of time and effort should bee spent on understanding and improving that other dimension.

Everyone has that third dimension. This is the dimension that defines our humanity. This is the dimension that allows us to dare, discover, love, reason, and appreciate the world around us. This is the dimension that provides us with the capability to control our behavior and appetites and make our senses a thing of pleasure rather than a means of survival. This third dimension allows us to live instead of merely existing.

To properly enjoy this third dimension, we must first of all recognize and appreciate its existence and then cultivate it. Each of us has great value. We have eyes to see, minds to think, and hands to help. Every one has something he can do well, and everyone has some deficiency to overcome. We all have something to contribute, and at sometime we all will need help. This third dimension will not just get better with age, in fact, without cultivation it can cause a lot of trouble. The appreciation of fine foods is part of this dimension, but without that cultivation, can be quite detrimental to good health and even good looks. The thrill of competition and the satisfaction of success can be most enjoyable, but it can foster greed and demand energies that should be used elsewhere. Our ability to invent can make our lives easier and exciting, but it must be used with moral restraint, because such ability can also hurt and destroy. We are unique inasmuch as we can love, but even this must be channeled into the proper directions or it can cause selfishness, heartache and jealousy.

In acres, depth is just as important as area. The real value of my acres is determined to a great extent, by what is below the surface. The texture of the soil, the drainage it affords, and the fertility, which determines what it will produce, all lie beneath the surface. In our lives, the true value is also that other dimension. Our value is not what can be seen at a distance or on the surface, but rather what is shown by our words and deeds and our contribution to all those around us. Acres of arid waste have little value, and so it is with shallow lives.

Rain

For my good earth to be productive, it must have moisture. It is needed for the seeds to sprout and for the roots to use the nutrients in the soil. Without this moisture, my soil is virtually worthless. This moisture comes from rain. It could come from rain falling a great distance away and channeled to fields by rivers and canals, it could soak through the soil into an aquifer and then pumped onto the fields, or as in my case, fall directly on the good earth. Everyone who tills the good earth knows the value and importance of rain. He also knows that rain is unpredictable. Sometimes it comes too late, sometimes it comes too hard, and sometimes too much falls.

When rain comes late, lawns turn brown and crops grow slowly or not at all. When rain comes too hard, the soil can crust and sprouting plants cannot emerge or come as hail and ruin the foliage. When too much rain falls soil can erode, lowlands flood, and rivers will overrun their banks and be very destructive forces. Rain, a necessity for anything to grow can also be most troublesome. Cloudy, gloomy, rainy days can be very depressing, that shower can ruin a picnic and wash out a ballgame and that rainstorm can be most frightening and even dangerous.

The wisdom of the ages tells us that "in every life a little rain must fall". This is usually interpreted as meaning we are all destined to have something bad happen once in a while. It should also imply that good things will also happen and even that the things that seem to be bad at the moment are usually opportunities for us to develop into a better person. It also should imply that the things that seem so good to us have a potential for harm. Like the rain, things never seem to come at exactly the right time or in the right amounts. Heartaches, disappointments, and even tragedy will happen to all of us, and these can either strengthen us or crush us, depending on reactions to them. Good things happen to all of us, too. There are those days when everything seems to go right, there are those friends and family to share interesting times, and sometimes even an extra dollar or two.

We must learn that we can't start or stop the rain, and it seldom comes in the right amounts at the right time, but dry spells always end and the rains always stop. We should learn that sometimes we might have to water the garden and we must always keep the roof repaired.

Spring

Every year has a winter. These are the weeks when the weather is cold, daylight hours are lessened, and close "hands on" contact with the good earth is limited. The cold weather freezes the good earth and sometimes even covers it with snow, making even necessary contact an unpleasant and difficult chore. The cold weather requires that we close the windows, seal the cracks, wear insulated clothing, and provide some heat. The sun is often hidden by clouds and at times fog hangs thick in the air. Sometimes roads are covered with ice and snow, even drifted completely shut and water pipes are often in danger of freezing. It is little wonder that we who are closely connected to the soil miss that closeness to it and anxiously look for the coming of spring.

Then spring does come, not in an instant, but rather a little bit at a time. There is an exact time when the astronomers say spring arrives, but the reality is that spring is a process. First, there are signs of spring. The days get a little longer and the sun hangs a little higher in the sky and its warmth can be felt even though the air might be cold and the ground still covered with snow. Seed catalogs come in the mail, icicles hang from the eaves and the good earth begins to thaw. Soon the robins arrive, crocuses bloom, and the pussy willows show a bit of gray on their bare branches. These are only signs, because the wind can still be cold, more snow will probably fall, and most of the trees and grass are still dormant.

This is a time for optimism and preparation. Seeds must be purchased, equipment readied, and plans for the summer are made. Even on cold days, the possibility of tomorrow being warm is real. After a cold morning, coats will probably be shed when the sun gets high in the sky. The warmer sun and the longer days finally dry up the mud, the good earth warms, and the grass begins to grow and buds form on the branches of the trees.

At last, the soil is ready for a garden to be planted. The soil is still too cold for everything, but peas, radishes, onions, and potatoes will sprout and grow and give an early harvest. Other things are starting to grow too. The willow is getting its leaves, the redbud is starting to bloom, and soon the rest of the trees will come to life. The amazing process of growth is evident all around. The great mystery of how these plants can turn dormant, survive the bitter winds of winter and spring to life when the heat from the sun gets sufficient, unfolds each spring and is a source of enjoyment and inspiration to those close to the soil.

This is also the time when "The Great Gardener" shows His handiwork. Every fencerow and woodlot has been seeded and will be covered with those wild and delicate flowers. The woods floor will be carpeted with spring beauties, violets will give a touch of color and nothing is more delicate than the Dutchman's breeches. This is a special time for a walk in the woods. There is even an early spring harvest. Those asparagus spears will soon appear and there will be morel mushrooms in the woods.

This is the start of a very busy season. Fields must be tilled and crops planted. This requires long hours when the weather permits. We like to envision spring days as always warm, bright and sunny, but that is not always the case. Between those ideal days, there are cold, wet, and windy days that can make work difficult and hard.

Each spring is an adventure in faith. Every spring is different from all others and weather patterns are never the same, but every year, winter changes into summer by the process we call spring. Though no two years are exactly alike and each year has its own identity, the earth does change from dormancy to life. The brown grass and bare trees will turn green. Seeds will be planted, the soil will get warm, the rains will come, the seeds will grow and there will be a harvest. Our guarantee of a summer is based on the history of the past and this is simply faith. Our lives are predictable in much the same way. We must review the past as a guideline for the future. We cannot know exactly what tomorrow will bring, but past experiences should provide for us a basis for a faith in the future and such faith is necessary for happiness. Spring is a time for optimism. We must believe that tomorrow will be an interesting, exciting, and happy adventure. No one is absolutely sure what will happen tomorrow or if tomorrow will even come, but it is to our advantage to believe that whatever happens we can cope with it and enjoy it.

Just as spring is a process, life is also a process. Rewards and consequences are future results of how we handle today. Both spring and life, are a series of ups and downs, the sun shines one day, and it snows the next, but on those snowy days, there is the certainty of sunny days ahead. This makes spring exciting. The lesson from spring should be the importance of faith and optimism. Without the promise and hope of sunny days, spring could indeed be a dreary time of the year, but that hope and promise can make any day exciting.

Our claim to life is only an instant, the moment we call now, and nothing makes that instant more enjoyable than faith and optimism. We cannot relive or change the past, we can only learn from it. We have no claim to the future; we can only plan for it. But we all have now and this fleeting moment must be lived to the fullest and used so that when it becomes yesterday, there will be nothing but happy memories and no regrets.

Planting Corn

In early spring, corn planters are a common sight working in the fields. Most of these are large complicated pieces of equipment, planting several rows at a time, and pulled by powerful tractors. I recall a time when such was not the case. Many years ago, I planted corn with a two row planter pulled by a team of horses.

That old planter was a very simple machine. It was simply two wheels that drove a chain that metered the seed, then covered the row so there would be good contact between the good earth and the seed and a marker to properly space the next two rows. You sat on a hard iron seat and guided the horses so that the tongue of the planter was exactly over the line you had just marked out. This sounds quite simple until you understand that getting off an inch or two would compound into a very crooked row after a short time and one of the criteria of a good farmer was how straight his corn rows were. Of course, horses didn't understand this, or care either.

I was a very young lad when I first planted corn with that old planter and my first attempts proved that I didn't qualify as a good farmer, if crooked rows were used as the definition. I sat on that hard seat and watched that mark as closely as I could and corrected and overcorrected and the results were very crooked rows and the harder I tried, the more crooked they became. It was then that dear old dad came to the rescue. Dad told me the secret of straight rows, or at least straighter rows. His magical advice was to look ahead. He told me that I should aim that planter tongue a long way down the field and that would take care of the little mistakes that the horses or me would make. It worked. The little mistakes that the horses or me would make only got larger until I sighted down the tongue and aimed ahead.

Thankfully, I gave up that old planter and those horses many, many years ago, but the knowledge of how to make straight rows remains and over the years as I have made connections with the good earth, it has become an important lesson in life. Whether it be straight rows of corn or a happy and successful life, you have to aim at some distant goal.

There is a remote possibility that I am much different than others, but my life seems to be plagued with a lot of little errors. There were times when I spoke when I should have remained quiet, and there were times when I should have spoken and didn't. There were times when I thought of myself at the expense of others. There were opportunities lost because of inaction and times I acted before I thought. There were times when I was too complacent and times when I was impatient. Please understand that in spite of these errors

I do not feel that I have completely wasted my life. While each of these weaknesses is worthy of mention, a higher and greater aim has used them as lessons for improvement. Also and needless to say, there are still a few kinks in my row.

The lesson here is that a morally successful life is something for which you can only aim. Those rows are never perfectly straight and there is always another row as a challenge. A little kink in a row will grow into a big kink unless it is straightened out with an aim in sight. A row, once planted cannot be unplanted and the errors sown into that row might not be noticed for awhile, but will be quite evident when the corn comes up. In life, there too is a day of reckoning.

Of course, there were the farmers who light-heartedly passed off their crooked rows with the explanation that you can get more corn in a crooked row, and mathematically they were correct. It was not that they were content with crooked rows or intentionally planted crooked rows, or were judging their neighbor's crooked rows, but rather as an excuse for their own little errors. They understood that, at that moment, perfectly straight rows were not an option and that they couldn't replant a whole field just to straighten a few crooked rows. All they could do was to make the best of it and try for better rows the next year.

I am very glad that I no longer plant corn with a team of horses, although that planter, was easy to repair, maintain and adjust. With the complicated machines that are seen working in the fields today, a working knowledge of mechanics, hydraulics, and even electronics is important. While such knowledge is valuable to plant corn today, it can never compare to my first lesson in corn planting; you get the kinks out of a row of corn by aiming ahead. You get the kinks out of life the same way.

Me & My Carrots

I am an amazing creation. I am not especially unique, but I can pull the weeds out of my row of carrots, and this is an amazing ability.

As a beginning, you have to know about my carrots. My row of carrots was planted early in the spring when the soil was quite cold. The carrots emerged rather slowly in that cold soil, but all sorts of weeds seemed to like that cold soil and emerged much quicker than the carrots. Also, when those carrots finally did emerge, they didn't even look like carrots. Mature carrot leaves are sort of lacy, but when the seeds finally came up, the first leaves were long and narrow and looked more like grass. Every carrot seed does not sprout at the same time, so there was a time when my row of carrots was a mixture of carrots with lacy leaves, carrots that looked like grass and weeds of all sorts and sizes. There comes a time when this mess must be sorted out and there seems to be no way but to get down on your knees, get your hands dirty, and pull out those weeds. This is one of those close connections to the good earth.

It was a very warm day in May. I had hoed out the weeds as close to the carrots as I could, but that left a long green strip of carrots and weeds across my garden. I got down on my hands and knees on that loose warm soil and started pulling weeds. My thoughts turned elsewhere. I could hear birds singing in the nearby trees and tried to identify them by their song. At the same time I was planning my work for tomorrow and considering some other projects for some later time. My thoughts strayed to family and friends and good times shared together. The sun was very warm and I was aware that I was sweating, getting thirsty and even a bit hungry. Then I realized that I was a living and working miracle.

My amazing mind could listen to the birds, plan for the future, recall and enjoy the past, and still sort out the many different kinds of weeds and pull them out of my row of carrots. My amazing mind

17

could size up each plant and determine whether it was a weed or a carrot while it was busy with other thoughts. It could sort the weeds from the carrots even when the leaves of the carrots themselves might be different. It could take a message from my eyes, determine any number of differences, co-ordinate my arms, hands and fingers and still allow me those other thoughts. It could sense heat and maintain a proper body temperature by producing sweat. [Note that when we are in contact with the good earth, we do not perspire, we sweat.] My amazing body could send a signal of thirst to replace the lost fluid and my body is capable of storing enough fluid so that it did not have to be constantly metered in. My amazing body sent messages that it could use some fuel, but that too, could be stored until a convenient time for a meal.

My mind can do a lot of other wonderful things. It can store a lot of experiences and recall them when I need them. It can add the experiences of others to my experiences and can take the sum of these experiences and use it to make reasonable judgements when new situations arise. I can receive communications from others, and share thoughts, ideas, and experiences in return. Because of these abilities, I have a responsibility to use my mind wisely. I must use past experiences to eliminate a regrettable present. My mind is also capable of great evil, so I must cultivate my thinking to be able to use it for my betterment and to help those around me. I must realize that all experiences will not be good and any good must be sorted from the bad. Using my mind properly is one of the keys to my happiness.

Whether we are weeding carrots or pondering the most complex problem, a miracle occurs and every one of us has access to that miracle. With such a wonderful gift, it seems only logical to feed it well and never abuse it with those chemicals that short circuit it for a moment of shallow pleasure. Our minds are a most wonderful blessing that can be a source of pleasure for a lifetime, and instead of wearing out, it just gets better with use. It is a great challenge to fill it with good thoughts and filter out those that can cause damage to you or those around you. It is a responsibility to share experiences when such sharing will be helpful, and it is a good idea to keep it open just a crack so that new ideas might enter and give new insights.

Whether it be weeding carrots or solving earth-shattering problems, your mind is a miracle and it would be foolish not to recognize it as such.

The Cathedral

It was a beautiful spring morning and I was plowing along the creek. The sun was just beginning to radiate some heat and its rays glistened through the drops of dew on the grass. The mechanical monster I was driving was proclaiming its power and the moist fertile soil was rolling over in its wake. To most, the scene would be an old farmer plowing a field, but in reality, it was a man worshipping in an outdoor cathedral among a small but friendly congregation.

The first members to appear were four deer. These friendly, but very shy, members stayed on the other side of the creek and quietly dined on the grass growing there. They were at peace with the world and felt secure and safe because of their keen eyesight, sense of smell, and speed if necessary.

The next members to arrive were a red tailed hawk and some red winged blackbirds. The hawk soared overhead looking for some movement on the ground that would provide a meal. Those other members, the blackbirds, who seemed to delight in pestering the graceful hunter, interrupted its hunting. The rowdy blackbirds chased and teased the larger bird almost as if it were a game.

The last members to arrive were some barn swallows. By some unknown instinct, they knew that a host of insects were stirred up by my activities and they were dining on those flying bugs.

My outdoor cathedral was decked with some fragile, but very beautiful flowers. Along the fencerow were violets, spring beauties, and Dutchman's breeches. The spring beauties formed a background of white by their sheer numbers, the violets gave a touch of color, and the Dutchman's breeches were as delicate as any orchid. It was not the Sabbath but how could this not be a time of worship? The cathedral was vast and decorated with green grass, trees starting to bud, and patches of blooming flowers. A congregation had assembled, and each member was sending a message of God's love and providence.

The deer, though timid and virtually defenseless, grazed peacefully and relied on their God given instincts for protection. Their sermon was that we all exist by the mercy of God and only by this mercy do we survive. The sermon from the hawk was of the virtue of labor. Although it's soaring seemed effortless, it had worked hard to gain that altitude and in spite of being hindered by the blackbirds, it persisted in its quest for food. The blackbirds' sermon was one of fun and enjoyment. Even if their enjoyment was at the expense of another, it was harmless and all too often, we take the nuisances of life too seriously. The lesson from the swallows was one of service, as they ate the insects that could harm my crops.

My friends, the rest of the congregation, were using their instincts and senses to survive, but I could appreciate beauty with mine. On that beautiful spring day, my labor was a labor of faith. I just knew that the sun would shine and warm the soil and that crops would grow. I just knew that rains would come and that if I planted good seed, fertilized and tilled properly, I would profit from my labor. This was also a time for thanksgiving. I was thankful for the privilege of worshipping in that wonderful cathedral. The dome overhead was maintained and well lighted both day and night. The gardens around the field had been planted by God himself and because of God's love; I was given the senses to enjoy the world around me rather than only surviving. I had been granted the ability to learn to use the good earth for my well being and I could share with others the priceless emotion of love that God had first shared with me. Although the noise of the tractor erased all other sounds, above it all, I could hear the chorus "How Great Thou Art".

Solitude

In the close association with the soil come many opportunities for solitude. In a crowded and fast moving world, solitude seems to be a rare adventure. To many it seems to be a condition to avoid at all costs because they mistakenly believe it is the same as loneliness. In reality, it could be a most precious time when the most important things in life can be pondered and sorted out.

That close association with the soil provides such opportunity. Planting seeds and pulling weeds while on hands and knees, times with shovels and hoes, and even on tractor and combine seats provide times when the greatest values in life can be addressed. What may be viewed as an opportunity by some could be seen as a burden by others, especially if life has unclear meaning and purpose. This is a time to mold personal philosophies and explore spiritual values. Sadly, this is overlooked by many and they would rather subscribe to values of others than formulate their own. They would rather read or listen than think and in so doing, are missing much. While the reading and listening is important, it can also be confusing, because for any idea expressed, there is an opposite one too.

While a close association with the soil offers many opportunities, moments of solitude are available to all. There is that time in an automobile when the traffic is light and the radio is turned off, those moments before sleep, or a walk by oneself, will work almost as well.

Moments of solitude should include a time of reverence and awe. We do live in an amazing world. This is a world of beauty. Skies, clouds, grass, trees, birds, flowers, and even people are items of beauty if we look for it. Beauty is all around, but because it is so common, we fail to see it and therefore to appreciate it until we are in danger of losing it. This is also a well-designed and smooth running world. It works very well without any intervention of mankind; in fact we seem more intent on destroying this marvelous creation than using it with respect.

Moments of solitude should be times when we meet ourselves. We should be brave and look upon ourselves as others see us. Are we observed as just an adorned body, or can others see some deeper values? We are each unique, yet we are so similar that all mankind share a certain brotherhood. We have many common grounds, we all feel hunger, thirst, pain, heat, and cold, and a smile and a frown are of a universal language. As we meet ourselves, we must ask ourselves who we really are. Are we the helpless infant who entered the world, the uncertain adolescent, the robust youth, the complacent adult, or the fragile elder? Any answer should indicate we are different persons at different times, but have a continuous thread that preserves our identity. We are more than body, we are soul.

Moments of solitude should be times when we seek purpose in life. We could view our existence as just an accident and drift aimlessly as a matter of survival. We could be self-centered and look at life as a challenge just to amass power, wealth, fame, or fortune. We could view our life as a life of servitude, either imposed on us or dedicated by ourselves to others. We could look on life as an adventure in danger and seek excitement and thrills. Probably, we see in ourselves a little of each of these purposes, if we are honest.

Moments of solitude must include dreams. No life is so perfect that it could not be better. There is tomorrow, and while there is nothing certain about it, it must be in our plans. Life must have an aim and steps to implement that aim, even when aims are of a preposterous nature and only for entertainment. Dreams rule out life's imperfections and unfairness and allow everyone to be a prince or a princess for a time. Without such moments, the sometimes harsh realities of life can become depressing, and who knows, dreams can come true.

I treasure my moments of solitude, because they give me moments to look at others. As I look at others, I can see my reflection and thereby my faults and weaknesses. When I am honest, I am able to see good and bad in everyone and because I am also human, can set a better standard to judge myself. It seems popular to believe that we are not to judge others, and to a point it is a worthy trait, so maybe the word evaluate is more apt. We all evaluate everyone we meet. We note physical appearance, personality, and attitude. We listen to ideas, opinions and adventures, and do form opinions of those we meet. I must confess that some of the people I meet, I like and some I would rather not be around, but these are times when I can cleanse myself of any tendency to abase, belittle and hate, and look for the good in others and note our similar weaknesses. Close examination will reveal that such thoughts are only self-destructive. These are times to strengthen bonds of friendship; times to reminisce, and times to relive those sacred moments spent with friends and family.

These are times I can meet my Creator. It is a time for repentance, thanksgiving, and worship. This can also be a time of great joy or great fear, in any case, a necessary and great challenge. Meeting our Creator is an eventuality for each of us, and a little familiarity gained in times of solitude just makes good sense.

My Friends & Acquaintances

During my adventure on the farm, I have met several creatures that have gained my utmost respect. Most of them I classify as friends, except one who is a despised enemy, but each of them has allowed me to appreciate my stay on this earth a little more.

First, my despised enemy. A short distance from my house was a pile of stones and broken concrete and over the years, it became the home of some groundhogs. They may have a good reputation as weather forecasters, but to me, they are very destructive little nuisances. They burrow under buildings and damage foundations and floors and seem to have few natural enemies. They dig holes in fields, ditch banks, and fencerows, and worst of all, they eat soybeans. From their burrows in field and fencerow, they come out to dine on soybean plants when they are first emerging. With their great appetites, their great numbers, and the fact that emerging soybeans are quite small, they can destroy a large area in a short time. For these reasons, they are an enemy to be destroyed.

Those groundhogs in that pile of stone were given the status of enemy number one and I kept my rifle handy so all I had to do was insert the clip, slowly and quietly open the door and shoot the little varmints. This is where the profound respect for them enters in. No matter how quietly I opened the door, no matter how quietly I inserted the clip, they could hear me and run for cover. Their ability to hear is almost unbelievable. For this ability to hear, they have my utmost respect and even some envy.

I have a friend that provides much entertainment as I work on my farm. I get to watch a red tailed hawk. It is either soaring high in the sky or sitting on a high limb of a tree watching me work or looking for some movement that will provide him or his family a meal. I have seen him dive from the sky or his perch and catch a mouse or a rabbit, and I cannot help but admire his keen eyesight.

Another friend is a big black lab that lives across the road. He had a rubber hamburger that would squeak when he bit it. He enjoyed that toy and would often carry it with him. One day, while hiking along a fencerow, he went along, carrying his rubber hamburger. Somewhere along the way, he got distracted and left his toy and returned home without it. Several days passed without his favorite toy, and then he went hunting for it. Somehow, after several days, he was able to pick up the scent of the trail he had traveled and locate his toy. As a test, his toy was placed on a grill that had recently been used, then hidden, and he was able to use his keen sense of smell to locate his toy hamburger in spite of the odors of the grill. I cannot help but admire his keen sense of smell.

On my farm, I have at times raised hogs. These creatures are noted for their good appetites, and to be raising profitably, these appetites must be satisfied. To do this, they get the same ration day after day. I also like to eat, but I also like a variety in my meals. Those hogs had a better-balanced diet than I ate, because the nutritional content of their meals was carefully considered. While I do consider nutrition an important part of eating, it is not the primary cause for my selection of food.

I have a big old cat. He is faithful, as cats go, and will follow me around as I work, and even curl up on my lap and purr. I am sure that somewhere in the neighborhood he has a family, but he assumes no responsibility for them or has any family ties to them. He is a pet who is driven by strong instincts and a strong desire for comfort, procreation, and self- preservation. Sometimes when life's responsibilities get a little heavy, his carefree life looks tempting.

My friends and acquaintances have taught me much about my role as a human being and an appreciation of the image of God created in me. While at times I may slightly covet the senses of my friends and acquaintances, deeper thought only turns my envy to pity.

That groundhog in the rock pile, even with that marvelous sense of hearing, cannot appreciate music. It can never understand a compliment, words of endearment, or any kind of communication. Sounds or words with his sense do not enrich his life he only survives.

My friend, the hawk, can see the mouse, but has no appreciation of a sunset, a flower, or green grass. He does not decorate his nest or follow any color scheme. His keen eyesight is only for survival.

The neighbor's dog is neither enticed nor offended by the aromas which bring pleasure to me. The aromas, freshly mowed grass, clover in bloom, the good earth, or dinner cooking, all associated with life on the farm, mean nothing to him. His almost uncanny sense of smell, even though for countless generations dogs have been domesticated, is only for survival.

My hogs are perfectly content with anything fed to them. Taste means little or nothing to them. Personally, I prefer a variety to my meals and taste makes mealtime most enjoyable. It makes the necessity for nutrition an enjoyment, not just a matter of survival.

My old cat has no idea of the emotion of love. He is faithful because I feed him. He cares nothing about any other cat. His love life is only for pro-creation.

The magnificent senses my friends and acquaintances have are only tools for their survival, while mine, even as poor as they may be, are for my enjoyment. When we were created, God shared with us the things that make life worth living. There is a world of beauty and adventure and we are to use it for our happiness, and we are wasting our life if we only use our God given senses to survive.

Erosion

Most of us who till the soil, recognize erosion as a problem. To those who are not so closely connected to the soil, the problem is most evident by muddy streams and rivers. It is that precious good earth that makes rivers and streams look brown, plugs up harbors and dams, is hard on wildlife, and makes water difficult to purify for municipal uses. To us who till the soil, it puts ruts in our fields and sends our topsoil down the river, and we understand the seriousness of this problem. We do many things to control this problem. We seed grass waterways, reduce tillage, and plant cover crops to keep our valuable topsoil from going down the river. Erosion is a serious problem, especially when the land is not flat.

Erosion occurs when water does not soak into the soil and runs over the surface. The amount of water, the texture of the soil, and the speed at which it runs over the soil determine the amount of erosion. The process of erosion starts very slowly; just a bit of moving water moves a grain of sand or a small particle of soil and carries it along. These particles are very small and would move very little, except that once loosened, they just keep moving as long as the water moves. The soil, something very solid, gives way to the water, something fluid, one little particle at a time until great damage is done, and once the soil is lost, it is gone forever.

Erosion is a slow process. Earthquakes and volcanoes can drastically change the topography in an instant. Whole mountaintops can be blown off or deep chasms formed by these destructive forces. Erosion happens one particle at a time, but these tiny particles can destroy with just as much certainty.

People can suffer erosion too. Just as there is good soil, there are good people, in fact, there is good in all people. There are several traits that determine the good in people. Good people are productive, responsible, trustworthy, and honest. Good people have learned certain values. By certain teachers, they have learned patriotism, neighborliness, morality, ethics, and spirituality. Once learned, these values make for very solid personalities, but there is always the danger of erosion. These learned values are never lost all at once, but rather can be lost one little grain at a time.

Good people seldom turn bad all at once. There is no earthquake or violent eruption that changes values or adherence to values with one shake or one blast. Good people seldom turn all bad. Erosion can happen in just one spot and all good people need to be on the alert for signs of erosion. It happens when good people compromise just a bit for expediency. It happens when one little lie is told and greater lies are needed to cover the first. It happens when business offers something just a little bit shady. It happens when a little bit of quality is sacrificed for a bit more gain. It happens when the wrong people influence thoughts and ideals. It happens when we forget to be thankful and become demanding. It happens when we become self-centered and spoiled. It happens when we replace God with many smaller gods.

Erosion is very subtle. It often occurs when things are going the best. It often happens when we are having fun. It often happens when there is opportunity for great success. It often happens when we are sure no one is looking or listening. It can even happen when we are with very nice people. It is often qualified by the notion "just this one time".

Every once in a while, I find that I need to make an erosion check. I profit from checking back to the values taught by, my parents and others who tried to instill time proven values into my life. I find it helpful to compare my actions and thoughts with the deeds and examples of those I admire, and to compare my actions and thoughts with the actions and thoughts that I expect of others. And while I am checking, although it is a bit scary, I try to check and make sure that there is no erosion in my relationship with God.

The thing that makes erosion so dangerous is that it is very hard to replace that good topsoil once it goes down the river. That good soil will never come back unless water will run uphill and return it, and that is not likely. Extra nutrients have to be added to compensate for those lost and measures must be taken to prevent further erosion. The respect of others, and a good name and reputation are in constant danger of erosion, and once gone, will be very difficult to repair. Common sense demands prevention.

There are many things that cause erosion in good people. The pursuit of popularity, greed, instant gratification, poor choice of friends, and carelessness are a few of the things that can cause any one of us to compromise just a little here and a little there. And just as that rut in the field develops by losing one tiny grain at a time, our values can be lost just one little bit at a time.

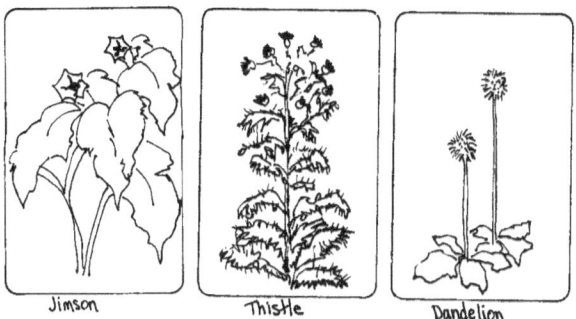

Jimson   Thistle   Dandelion

Weeds

A lot of my close contact with the good earth has been caused by unpleasant things, in fact, the whole adventure of life seems to be beset with some unpleasant things, and how we deal with this segment of life, to a large extent determines our state of happiness. These unpleasant things can depress us or teach us valuable lessons, tear us down or strengthen us, master our lives or be a window of opportunity. Weeds are such a thing.

Weeds always seem to grow and when you are tilling the good earth, they provide a constant foe. One of the basic rules of all agriculture is that a growing crop needs sunlight, moisture, and the nutrients found in the soil, and the competition for these elements must be eliminated, therefore, for a bountiful crop, weeds have to be destroyed. There are several ways to fight weeds. Modern agriculture has developed chemical sprays that work well on large areas, but there was a time and there are places where that is not an option. There was a time and there still are conditions when they must be dug out with cultivators and hoes and even pulled out by hand. This hands on contact with the weeds can teach some valuable lessons.

There seems to be a never-ending supply of weeds. You dig them up or cut them down and they just keep coming. To a certain extent, you can thin them out by constant cultivation, but they never seem to be eliminated. They have too many ways of sneaking into a field or garden. Sometimes a seed can stay in the good earth for years before it sprouts. Sometimes a little piece of root is all it takes for a weed to get started. Sometimes they blow in on the wind. Always, when a weed is not destroyed, it will produce a lot of seed for another generation. The ability to survive in so many ways and in so many places is what makes them weeds.

In my battle with the weeds, several have gained my utmost respect, and over the years, except in one case, there has been no clear-cut victory on either side. These weeds are controlled enough so that they do little damage to my crops, but they never are eliminated. I never can say that I have won, because they have the potential to be back next year. I can win the battle, but never the war.

I have four "favorite" weeds. One must always respect the enemy and in my battle against these four, they have gained my utmost respect. One weed has no economic impact on me, one weed, usually unrecognized, I have actually conquered, another appears every time I think I have won, and the last is the most subtle fighter of the group. Each of them has a different plan of attack and so the battle strategy must be different for each. Allow me to introduce my foes, their plan of attack and my offense.

In my yard, dandelions always grow. They do not interfere with any field crop and therefore have no economic impact at all on me. If you pick one little yellow flower and look closely at it, it would not appear out of place in a flower garden, and many children have picked bouquets of them and many mothers have appreciated the attention. To the innocent eyes of a child, they are a beautiful flower. Even when they are ripe, the white winged seeds are most delicate and who hasn't blown on them to see the little white parachutes fly? The plants are even edible, so why is this innocent appearing plant such an enemy? If these delicate little yellow flowers would stay in a flowerbed, they might be well liked, but they don't. Those little white parachutes carry a very fertile seed, and that seed will grow almost anywhere, and once started will put down a long taproot and it is almost impossible to destroy. This makes it a hated weed. A thing of beauty with even a practical value, becoming a pest because of shear numbers and appearing in unwanted places.

There was a time when one of my most valuable crops was a weed. This is the battle, which I have won. There was a time when there always seemed to be a lot of waste when harvesting corn because the available equipment just was not very efficient. This wasted corn would survive the winter and grow the next spring and become a real weed in soybeans following the corn. The corn would compete with the beans for sunlight and moisture, reducing the yield. At harvest the corn would ripen at the same time as the soybeans and could not be easily separated at harvest. Here was a very good thing appearing at the wrong time and at the wrong place. Better harvesting equipment and chemical weed control has allowed me to win this battle.

One of my more formidable enemies is jimson weed. This is a late summer weed that can grow five or six feet tall and produce thousands of seeds inside a thorny burr. This weed stinks and to anyone stupid enough to try it, is hallucinogenic and possibly poisonous. A field may look weed free until late summer and then these weeds will appear. The seeds are capable of staying in the soil and sprouting after many years, so just when you think you might have won, they will pop up again. The seed is there just waiting for one little lapse of attention and the battle has to start all over.

Another weed that puts up a good fight is the Canada Thistle. Winged seeds can spread these weeds, but a real battle begins when a patch gets established. They will spread through their roots. One little piece of root is capable of growing into a very large patch in a hurry and roots go deep and can spread over a large area. A battle against this underground foe is seldom completely won.

We all have weeds in our lives. These are little battles against things that will make us unproductive, unattractive, unpleasant, and unlikable, or if unattended, even evil. These are constant battles that we just don't seem able to win. We can gain for a while and think we have won, but when we get a bit careless, we have to fight again and if we do win a battle, we never win the war.

There are those dandelions. They can be harmless, even pretty and practicable, until they get in the way of things of greater value. They can be good in their place, but they soon crowd into places they are not wanted. It can be work, play, entertainment, or even acts of charity that interfere with family, health, or things of spiritual value.

There is that corn growing where and when it shouldn't be. Wealth, influence, and education are important to a happy useful life, but can be used for selfish or wrong purposes. These crops that are nurtured and valuable can foster arrogance and provide competition for time that should be spent on other valuable crops.

There are those jimson weed seeds that get planted deep within our hearts and souls. They are the habits and mistakes of bygone days that often provide temptations long after the battle is thought to be won. These weeds can be poisonous to our souls.

Then there are those thistles. These are weaknesses that grow deep and are almost impossible to destroy. Hatred, intolerance, and arrogance, which are deep rooted by culture and education, grow deep and are hard to kill.

Any of these weeds can be quite a formidable foe. If not recognized and controlled, single plants will spread into large patches, and whole patches are almost impossible to eradicate. I have found these little weeds in my life are always waiting for a bit of carelessness or inattention. There always seems to be some seeds blowing in from somewhere that will sprout quickly if ignored. It would indeed be foolish if I would wait until the weeds were mature and caused a lot of damage before I considered destroying them. It isn't easy, but if you get down on hands and knees and get in close contact with that soil, they can be cut off or pulled up, one at a time whenever they appear. The threat of dandelions, jimson, and thistles will never go away, but if we are to live up to our potential, they must be controlled.

Green Apples

In our area, most of the farmsteads were established in the late 1800's. This is when the big barns were built, family sized houses built, fields fenced, and orchards planted. It is these orchards that I am considering now, especially the apple trees. These apple trees were important as they provided a fruit that could be eaten in season, stored for the winter, and as a source for vinegar which was used as a preservative. These apple trees were not the dwarf variety that is most common today, but would get quite large, and these big old apple trees were an interesting part of my childhood.

Me, and the other farm kids that I grew up with liked to climb. We would climb up on the big beams in the barn, swing on the hay ropes, and climb trees, and those old apple trees were ideal for climbing. There were usually some low limbs, which made them pretty easy to climb, and then there were the apples.

You could climb these trees and eat apples, and for some reason we would eat these apples before they were ripe, and this was not always a wise thing to do. Too many green apples have a very bad effect on a young digestive system; this was a known fact. Our parents warned us and even past experience confirmed it, but still, every once in a while, we would get a bellyache from eating green apples. An immediate reaction would be, stupid kids, or I warned you, or why would anybody do such a thing, and that is an interesting question, "Why would anyone do such a thing"?

Why would a kid climb a tree and eat green apples? They were sour and not very tasty. We were not starving or even hungry. There was no medicinal value. We were properly warned as to the effects by parents or experience, but still, on occasions we ate green apples.

One justification was that there is not a distinct line between ripe and green apples. Ripening is a process and the apples get sweeter and better tasting a little bit at a time, and it is possible that the apples might be almost ripe, but almost ripe apples are not likely to cause too much discomfort.

Impatience might be the answer. They did taste a little like the ripe fruit and maybe, just maybe, it was a sort of impatience. A better reason was concealed in the fact that there was usually more than one kid involved. Few kids were by themselves when they ate too many green apples. There was a sort of peer pressure or daring involved in eating those sour apples. Who would be so bold to admit that those apples were too sour or that his digestive tract was not up to the challenge of a few green apples?

We all knew that just one apple would have no effect, but no one seemed to know how many would. Our parents warned us about eating too many, but never defined how many that really was.

There was no specific family law concerning this matter, at least not until after some one got a bit sick, and we were pretty sure the rules for one year did not necessarily carry over to the next.

This might seem like kid's stuff, but most adults "eat a lot of green apples". These are things that by adult logic and intelligent reasoning should not be done. We could begin with food consumption and other things we ingest, and these are important, but there are other important "green apples". These are the things that have serious consequences to our well being or cause unhappiness, heartache, and guilt. These are the things done because of impatience, peer pressure, or desire for instant gratification. These are the things that can be excused because there was no law against it or "it didn't hurt anyone", or lack of a pure definition of "green". These are things that we are sure will not affect us "this one time". These are things that we should avoid because of past experience or from observing others. These are not necessarily the big sins in life, kids very seldom if ever died from eating green apples, but are those things which pose a hazard to our minds and physical bodies or little things that make us less loveable to those around us and to God.

I admit that I ate my share of green apples, and also admit that as an adult, I still do some things I know I shouldn't do. Instead of my belly aching, it is my heart or someone else's that is hurt. I have found that life is not all "cut and dried" and that there are "shades of gray" and that often words are used in a clumsy manner and cause pain. At times I have been impatient and acted without considering all of the facts or all of the consequences. I must admit that I am at times influenced by peer pressure and fail to take a positive stand or allow a wrong to go unchallenged. I have found that there are times when my accepted rules for living just don't seem to apply, and when the lesser of two evils must be considered.

Our world is full of apple trees, and loaded with green apples. While we could just sit in the shade and look up at the apples, or just stand back and watch the neighbor kids have fun climbing the tree, but most of us like to get into the action. We find this action whenever we are part of a family, doing business, or interacting with society. It is hard, but we must always remember that those green apples can cause much pain and discomfort.

The Well

It was a lovely May day, and I was plowing some thick clover sod behind the barn. I had tilled this field for many years and believed that I was quite familiar with all of it. The field was gently rolling which caused a great variation in soil texture and color. Watching the various types of soil roll over, the fragrance of the soil, and the enjoyment of the great outdoors made this a most pleasant job. My attention was drawn to an unusual hole in the ground in the furrow ahead, and I thought it to be worthy of some investigation. My first impression was that a groundhog had been digging, and due to a hatred for the destructive little beast, it was a good excuse to get off the tractor, stretch my legs, and take a good look at that hole.

It was hard to believe what I found. Instead of just a little hole, it was a big hole and I could not even see the bottom. This was most unusual. I got a shovel and dug around and discovered the hole was an old well. Over the years, I had driven tractors, combines, and all sorts of heavy equipment over that spot and never had any hint of anything unusual. It still remains a mystery as to why some heavy piece of equipment hadn't fallen into that hole, but there it was, an old well in the middle of my field. This well was about three feet in diameter, lined with stones and was over ten feet deep; this needed further investigation and some extra hands. It was time to call the family in.

We needed a long ladder, a strong rope, a bucket, and a shovel. I went down that ladder, not knowing what might be at the bottom. We discovered that at sometime, someone had thrown some trash in the well, but could find no remains of any kind of cover. We filled the bucket, hauled it up, and filled it again and again, but even after several such sessions in the well have not found the bottom or any water.

To me, this well is a lesson in appreciation of my heritage and a monument to some unknown pioneer heroes. These heroes were everyday people doing what was necessary to make a living under far from ideal circumstances. I do not know their names, but a little imagination tells quite a story. This area was settled a little over 150 years ago. It was covered with thick forests of oak, hickory, and maple, it sold for $1.25 per acre. For that $1.25, all a person got a piece of paper declaring him owner. There were no roads and there were no stores, mills, or markets within miles, and no close neighbors. You probably didn't have even a horse until you could clear the forest and raise some hay and pasture. You also did not have any water. From this well, the nearest dependable water supply, that is a creek that ran all summer, was over two miles away.

Probably, several hardy people got together to build a log cabin that would shelter them until some logs could be sent to a sawmill and a better house built. They had to till the good earth around stumps in order to raise the grain to provide their food. And they had to get water. I can only imagine the work entailed in digging the well. Digging a hole four and a half feet in diameter is hard enough if it is only five or six feet deep. Then it gets so deep that the dirt has to be put in a bucket and lifted to the surface, the work would be very hard and slow. Then there is the constant danger. Even in our hard clay, those walls could cave in, and the possibility of a rope breaking or slipping with a bucket of dirt high above your head would always pose a hazard.

This well was lined with stones. These stones were probably found in the surrounding fields. One can only imagine the work required to carry these stones to the site, and that was just the beginning. They no doubt had to dig that well until they found water and then start lining the hole from the bottom up. The idea of those 25 pound and sometimes larger, stones lowered to a worker in the well would be cause for concern. Digging this well was slow, difficult, and dangerous.

Too often, we overlook the real heroes that made our life so easy. We read of explorers and are impressed with their daring, we hear of entrepreneurs who founded industry and appreciate their foresight, we study about soldiers and their feats of valor in times of war, but overlook the everyday people who carved out the farms and villages in early America.

These pioneers went into unknown lands, risked their meager savings, and confronted the dangers that life on the frontier imposed and we do not even know their names. They lived in crude cabins until by the sweat of their brow, they could build better, and then built roads, mills, schools, stores, and churches and formed local governments. They were independent, but knew the importance of neighbor helping neighbor, valued freedom, but understood responsibility, and were not afraid of hard work. We could learn much from them.

To some, my well might be just a hole in the ground, but to me it is a monument. It is a monument to a vision of something better that was not deterred by danger or hard work. It is a monument to independence that came with the price tag of risk and discomfort. It is a monument to success. That water possibly was not as pure as we are accustomed to have and definitely not as handy as just turning a faucet, but I bet it tasted mighty good on a hot afternoon. It sure beat carrying water from a creek two miles away, too.

It is too bad every school child doesn't have to dig just a little hole, so that they would appreciate the wonderful heritage that is handed to them on a silver platter.

Change

Everyone experiences changes, but we who have close connections to the good earth possibly get a little different angle to change than most. Many people resist change, fear change, or fail to understand change and because of this accept a lesser status in life than they should. Others want to change everything and miss much by failing to appreciate things as they are. In a fast moving world, it is quite appropriate to study change and learn to accept change as an eventuality.

Contacts with the soil are motivated by changes. Seeds are planted with the sole purpose of their changing. A good seed will change quickly. It will absorb moisture, the miracle of germination will occur, a sprout will emerge, a root will probe into the soil, and a stalk will seek the sun. This plant will constantly change as it grows and eventually the changes will produce a seed of like kind and fulfill the purpose of its planting. Such change is expected.

Some other changes are necessary. Cold soil must get warm, dry soil must get moist, wet soggy soil must dry out, and seasons must change. The sun must shine, but rain clouds are also needed. We know these changes will occur, but are to a point unpredictable, and often come too little or too late, but they always come. Every drought has ended with rain and every flood has receded, every cold spell has warmed up and every heat wave has subsided, and even every beautiful day has had its sunset. Over these changes we have no control, except to adapt, and often feel frustration when they pose danger or inconvenience but experience teaches us to adapt.

Times change also. Political boundaries seem to always change, different social problems emerge, and customs and manners appear to change with each generation. Technology causes an acceleration of change and the ethics to properly use these changes often lag behind.

People change. Children mature, adults get old, and even dreams, goals, and ideas do not always remain the same. Some of this change is from natural causes, and some from experience or environment.

Our environment changes. My boyhood home is now a subdivision and the fields and woods that I had the privilege to wander and explore are no longer open to other little boys for such adventure. The small towns, where I at one time did most of my business, have lost many of the local merchants and business and industry has grown large and impersonal and often far away. Cities have expanded their boundaries and their sprawl has given rise to miles of highways to handle the increased traffic. In our demand for all sorts of luxury and convenience, we have been hard on our natural resources, polluted our air and water, and not yet properly solved the problem of getting rid of our waste safely.

Change is neither good nor bad. Change is a constant thing and how we adapt to this eventuality is of most importance. We who are associated closely with the soil, understand that there are three kinds of changes, those we willfully make, those over which we have only a limited control, and those of which we have no control.

I, by conscience effort, change many things. The growth of crops and livestock is expected and our success or failure is determined by our ability to control this growth. We breed our livestock selectively, feed with care and provide a proper environment for health and safety, understanding that such care will make favorable changes. We plant good seed, cultivate, and fertilize, and harvest in a timely fashion, and know the necessity of such care if our crops are to be profitable. In each case, we expect change and do our best to control that change.

We have very limited or no control over many other changes. There is the weather, prices, and people. At times, not only do we have to sit by and watch for these changes, but also sometimes sit by hoping for a change. We know that the weather will eventually change, but so often, we get very impatient. It can be just a matter of comfort or inconvenience, but that flood or tornado can even be a matter of life or death. On one of those perfect June nights, we often wish we could preserve it forever but the good changes as well as the bad. We understand that weather will change, but until it does, we must adapt. Often we get impatient in the workplace. We want that change, maybe a promotion or salary increase, or maybe fear a change, a job loss or other uncertainty, and over this we only have limited control. We can establish a good work record or pursue further education, but there are many factors beyond our control. Then, there are people. We watch that child grow and develop, and are anxious for that first step, or first word, or progress to another grade, but then feel a certain apprehension when they are old enough to drive or have that first date. We watch helplessly as friends or family make moral or social mistakes and wish for a character change, or watch that person with those personal problems and hope that his "luck" will change. We have very limited control over other people.

At some time in everyone's life he will notice that he is changing. There is that physical change that just happens. A body will mature and develop and eventually fade and sort of waste away, and aside from the influence of good rules of health, it will just happen. Education and experience will cause a mind to develop, change, and assume responsibility. While we think it might be a good thing to be

40

able to change others, we do have the option of changing ourselves. This is a most important option. None of us are so good that we should not always be trying to improve ourselves just a little bit.

Each of us will change as we mature. Experience, environment, society and opportunities will present many challenges as we face these changes, and it is our responsibility to be sure that these changes are for the better. We are at the mercy of many of these changes, but we do have the choice to accept or adapt and how we handle these changes will to a large extent determine our happiness.

Collision

One of the things I learned at a very young age, about the good earth, is that it is hard and falling on it can be quite painful. Because it is painful, it has been a good teacher of several lessons. Words of advice were not always apt for every occasion or sometimes got ignored, but a little bit of pain goes a long way in making a point. Collisions with the good earth have taught me several good lessons.

One lesson was to watch where you step, especially if the good earth is frozen. I gained a very sore knee by stepping on a patch of icy frozen ground. It is always good sense to watch where you step, since life has a lot of slippery spots and falls from them can be pretty hard too. The trouble with slippery spots is that you don't fall down every time, in fact, most of the times when we tread on dangerous ground we escape collision. Sore knees soon heal, but broken hearts, wasted lives, and tarnished honor heals much slower, if at all.

A long time ago, when I was yet in grade school, we had a ball diamond right behind the school that provided us with an opportunity for a lot of fun. It was not a well-manicured diamond like most kids play on today, but rather a makeshift affair with some serious defects. One of the major defects was a lot of coarse gravel around third base. This was no real problem unless you were lucky enough to get to third base and unlucky enough to have to slide. If ever you had to slide, that gravel would do a number on whatever part of your body hit the good earth. It was also hard on clothing. Once in a while, there came that split second in your life to decide whether to slide or not to slide, or in more mature terms, consider the consequences to your actions. There were some that would rather be out than slide under those conditions, but most would risk getting skinned up if they thought they would make it. While the decision to slide was not a momentous decision of worldwide consequences, decisions of worldwide consequences do carry great risk. Lands were never explored or fortunes made by people who refused to take a risk. On the other hand, nothing was ever worth taking foolish chances. The lesson from the ball diamond is that risks are part of the adventure of life, and the dangers involved must be carefully calculated.

The greatest lesson I learned from collision with the good earth involved our old bicycle. During the '30s times were hard and few luxuries were to be had. One day, my father brought home an old used bicycle, and, of course, there were a lot of contacts with mother earth in the process of learning to ride the thing. It was much too large for a person as little as I was. I could barely reach the pedals and couldn't come close to sitting on the seat, but it was a bicycle and it served the purpose.

We lived on a hill with a ravine on either side and to get any distance from home, it was necessary, first to go downhill, that was easy, and then to go uphill, that was hard. To have any chance at all of getting up the hill, you had to get a fast start down the hill, and then, possibly, you could make it all the way up the hill.

There were a couple other things that might be hard for those not living in that era to understand. Our road was just a gravel road. This meant that along each side of the road and down the middle the gravel was loose and getting into that loose gravel probably meant a wreck. The other thing was that old bicycle had no guard over the chain, and no guard over that chain allowed, yes even encouraged, pants legs to get tangled in it. Some of the richer boys had a metal clip that they could put around their pants leg, but all we did was to roll up one pant leg high enough to keep it out of the chain. Whenever your pants leg got caught in the chain you were helpless, especially if you were so short your feet wouldn't touch the ground. You had to get stopped somehow and back that chain off enough to get loose. It was very hard on pants and small bodies too, because stopping a bicycle under those conditions was a disaster. Now consider this equation. A small boy on a large bicycle riding as fast as he can down a hill on a gravel road so he can make the next hill, an unguarded chain and he forgot to roll up his pants leg. The answer, his pants get caught in the chain, he hits the loose gravel, he looses control, and boy, bicycle, and stones get all tangled up, and that hurts.

In today's world, the boy's parents get a lawyer. They sue the county for having loose gravel on the road, the manufacturer of the bicycle for not guarding the chain, and the maker of the pants for not having anything on the label citing the danger. They also take

43

the scratched child to an emergency room to see if there were any broken bones. I didn't even get any sympathy. Some iodine would be put on my scratches and a little tape if necessary, the bicycle would be checked for damages, and I would be told to be more careful the next time.

Were my parents cruel? Of course not. They knew that it hurt, but that those scratches would soon heal. They also understood that in this dangerous world it was my responsibility to take care of myself. They knew that bicycle, like any other pleasure had certain dangers. They also knew that I knew how to prevent such an accident from happening and just didn't take the necessary precautions.

Please understand that I am not advocating that every parent take the chain guard off their children's bicycle just so they can learn responsibility for their safety the hard way, there are better ways, but that old bicycle was effective.

There seems to be some notion that the world can be made completely safe and every accident is the fault of someone else. This is evident, not only in mechanical things, but also with things social and moral. My experiences in life have convinced me that there are slippery spots, third base might have some stones around it, and every bike does not have a chain guard, but it is still fun to walk when it is icy, play ball, and ride a bicycle. I also believe that you will also miss much if you wait until all the ice melts before you go outside, spend too much time picking up all the stones around third base, and wait until you can afford a new bicycle with a chain guard. My contacts with the good earth have taught me that a few nicks and scrapes are part of life and they should teach good lessons in responsibility.

The Creek

There is something about water that connects to young boys. Sometimes, it is the fish that are in it, sometimes it is actually getting into it, and sometimes it is simply mixing it with the good earth and playing in it. Sometimes this water is in puddles, which are never to be avoided. Other times it is in ponds or lakes, prompting the need for something to float. Often times it is flowing and needs exploration. Then there is the bathtub, which seems to be a waste of time because a person just gets dirty again.

As a boy, a lot of fond memories are associated with creeks. We had a small one that ran through our woods on a part time basis. It wasn't spring fed and except for some of the deeper spots, dried up in the summer. That little creek went from our woods across several fields and crossed the road just down the road from our house. These small bodies of water were a constant attraction. There were always frogs to hunt, and even at times some small fish would venture into the deeper areas. These creeks always needed some exploration, and this often required that shoes and socks be removed and pants legs rolled up and it seemed no matter how high they were rolled, it was always one roll too short.

As an adult, I bought a farm, and this farm has a creek running through it. It is a beautiful little creek with trees on both sides and it flows even during dry spells. I have given up hunting frogs, and even wading, but walking along the creek is still a great pleasure. There always seems to be a duck or heron in the water, a deer or rabbit getting a drink, and there seems to be enough little boy in me to enjoy watching water running over the rocks.

My creek runs for over a half mile through my farm. One day, as I was walking along my creek, I noticed some red flags tied to some stakes. This was quite upsetting, because I knew why those flags were there. Everyone does not call my pretty little stream a creek. On official records, it is called a county drain, and because it is a drain, the county has the responsibility to keep it free of debris and keep it free flowing so as to allow drainage for the surrounding fields. The flags were an indication that some work was going to be done on my creek.

I had paid for my creek and could enjoy it, I could harvest timber beside it, and I could plant crops beside it. Besides buying it, I paid taxes every year on it, but in spite of my ownership, the county could come in and do whatever they wanted to do to it. They had legal access to seventy feet on either side of my creek, or about five acres of my land. They could destroy any crops planted there, cut any tree growing there, and remove any fence or bridge that was in their way. The point here is not of protest, but rather to stimulate some thoughts on true ownership.

The question raised is whether it is my creek or someone's drain or both. As my creek, it is a place of beauty, and a place to recall happy boyhood hours. It is a place that I have bought with hard earned money and on which I perform my civic duty and pay taxes. It is a place where I can invest time and money and plant a crop and profitably use, except for rare times of repair and maintenance. As my creek, I can harvest the trees along the banks and hunt game or fish. As a drain, it truly belongs to someone else and I only have the use it. It is subject to the greater good of those of the watershed and the rules pertaining to it are very plain. Whether it is my creek or any other part of our world, there is always a question of ownership. No mater what legal document we may possess, or price we may think we have paid, we never own any part of this world. We may have a creek, profitably use it, enjoy its beauty, and even transfer such rights to others, but in a relatively short time, we surrender all rights to it and it becomes a drain, We are only stewards.

I know that I will not own my creek eternally, but while I do, I have a responsibility to take care of it. I hope that there will be some other little boys that want to wade in my creek and hunt frogs and get their feet muddy. I also hope that these little boys will grow into men with happy memories of my creek and also understand who really owns the creek.

Fences

There was a time when almost every farm had livestock, and if you had livestock, you had fences, and when you had fences, they always needed repairs. Livestock always seemed to have the uncanny ability to find any weak spots in a fence and if they couldn't find one, they would make one. There were always those emergency repairs that had to be made just at supper time or when you were dressed to go away, but a lot of the fence fixing was one of those jobs you did when there was nothing to do. Fixing fences was hard work and often required digging a hole when the good earth was dry and hard. For a kid on the farm, fixing fences was not a favorite job, even though he was a sort of expert by reason of experience.

One fine Sunday morning, I was setting in church. As a teen-age boy, there were several places I would rather have been at that moment, even though it was not an option. I was getting restless and a bit hungry, so I was watching the clock pretty close, so I knew that the preacher was lasting a bit long. My thoughts were everywhere except listening to anything he had to say. I sort of came to attention when I heard him say something about fixing fences. I knew that the preacher had no past experience on a farm, and I couldn't imagine what he could tell me, an experienced farm boy, about something that I was more expert than he was. He told this story.

He said that a farmer had hired a man to build a fence. The man went out and labored all day and came to the farmer that night for his pay. The farmer asked the man how things went, and the man replied that on the average, things went pretty well. This concerned the farmer, so he asked the man what he meant by "on the average".

The man said that the fence was not easy to build. Some places the land was level, but other places there were hills and places covered with brush and thorns. He said that he couldn't do a very good job on the hills and through the brush and thorns, so he built the fence on the flatland extra strong, so on the average, the fence was good.

Possibly, no one else in that congregation really knew what that fence was worth as well as I did. I knew exactly what would happen the first time cattle were turned in that field. The cattle didn't understand averages, but they did understand weak spots in a fence, and despite hills and thorns, they were going to get out. It only takes one weak spot to make a fence worthless.

The city preacher's message to a country boy was well made. You have to mend the weak spots in your life. You do not better yourself by enhancing your strong points, but rather, you get better by repairing those hard to reach weaknesses.

You don't see many fences anymore, unless they are painted white to look fancy, or chain link to guard something, or a single electric wire, but there was a day when every farm had a lot of fences and their maintenance was an important part of farm life. They were either to keep something in or something out, and for the same reasons, all of us need fences in our lives. There are all sorts of things that need to be kept out. Some theologians have counted them and say there is seven deadly sins and I would never argue about the number, but I do know that there are several out there that need a strong fence to keep them out. There are times in all our lives when we need such protection. Early lessons of right and wrong, the lessons taught by experience and adventures, and what we should learn by observing the best in society around us, are things that must be protected from urges for instant gratification or sold for the price of popularity or power.

There are things that need fenced in. Those dark thoughts and angry words that can harm should not escape. Gossip and unkind words also need very strong fences at times.

Whether we are fencing something in or fencing something out, an average fence should never do. The weak spots need to be rebuilt. In even a greater sense, we dare not be content with being average. If we know one person who has less than average moral or ethical standards we have an obligation to have above average standards to even maintain a society as it is at present, let alone make the world better. Simple mathematics tells us that. Our challenge should be to do our share to make this old world a better place, if for no other reason than making it a better place for the next generations.

This world is full of unlikely teachers. It isn't very often you get a good and lasting lesson from something as unpleasant as fixing fences, especially, if you are sure the teacher doesn't really know what he is talking about.

The Road

I live on what many call a dirt road. Many years ago it was surveyed as a division of land and cleared of forest. No doubt, for many years it was little more than a trail of mud, ruts and dust, but now the county maintains it and it is well graded and covered with gravel. This road really goes nowhere. It does not provide access to any industry, or is it a thoroughfare between cities, or even a short cut between busy places, it is just a short road with a few houses along it. Since it is not paved, it gets dusty in summertime, muddy in the spring, and sometimes gets a little rough. There have been times when winter snow has drifted it shut and since it is just a little country road, has kept us snowbound for several days. These features of my road would seldom be used as assets for my property, but I like my road.

Since my road doesn't go anywhere, it is sparsely traveled and that allows me to recognize almost every vehicle that uses it. Most of the traffic is neighbors and these neighbors will wave as they go by, and even stop and talk at times. Our neighborhood is not nosy, but we are well enough acquainted to be concerned about each other's welfare. We can help when needed, are on hand in emergencies, and can share concerns and pleasures. My road promotes good neighbors.

Traffic on my road is rather slow. I can walk across with no fear and it is very rare that I have to wait for any traffic to pass. Kids can ride bicycles and chase a ball safely. I can even take a walk down my road at night and not be noticed, with the possible exception of a neighbor's dog and I know all the dogs well enough to pet them. In a fast moving world, it is nice to live on a quiet and safe country road.

My road allows me to contact the rest of the world. I am not isolated. It is an access to towns and cities where I do my business, and buy my supplies. It makes possible for the mail and newspapers to come to my door and other deliveries to be made. My road allows me to contact friends and relatives and for them to visit me, it makes my business and social life convenient.

Most important, it is the way home and my home is a very special place. It is more than just the house I live in; it is the center of my life. It is not the place I go after work, but rather the place I leave to go to work, and there is a vast difference. It is where my family is, whether it is spouse or children or visiting children and grandchildren. It is where my family can have meals together, share the good and bad in life with one another, and laugh and tease and enjoy each other. It is where I can take off my shoes and prop up my feet and wear clothes just because they are comfortable. It also reflects my tastes in its decoration and style. It extends beyond my house, because this is also where I can have gardens, and lawns, and trees, and flowers and have room to play and relax.

My old dirt road leads to the heart and center of my love. Over the years and at various times, I have had the opportunity to express, sometimes awkwardly or insufficiently, my love for my spouse and my offspring. The arms of a loving spouse, a hug from the little arms of a child, and other expressions of love are the things that put the greatest meaning in life. This is also the spot to share dreams, mend broken hearts, and conquer the everyday problems of life.

It's just an old dirt road, but it leads to the center of the greatest values on earth. A super highway may be an engineering masterpiece, but until it leads to such a destination as my old dirt road, it is but a monument to superficial values and those values are very limited.

Harvest

Most of my contacts with the good earth are enjoyable and with one purpose in mind. Whether it be tilling, planting, or cultivating, it was done with a harvest in mind. There is always a harvest, sometimes it is good, sometimes it is poor, but always something. In pursuit of this harvest, there are a few absolutes, but there are many more probabilities than absolutes involved in this connection with the soil.

One thing that is absolute is that when I plant grains of wheat, I get wheat, never corn or anything else. Even though my understanding of the process of germination is very limited, I do know that I can absolutely depend on getting wheat when I plant wheat. I also know that I can depend on the seasons changing. There will be a winter and a summer. How cold it will get in the winter, or how hot it will get in the summer, I can never be sure, but I can depend on a change of seasons. I also know that the sun will shine, there may be clouds that may hide it for a time, but I just know that it is up there and shining brightly. These are the most obvious absolutes.

Most of the other connections are probabilities and over which, I have a little bit of control. I can plant good seed, and cultivate as necessary, and eliminate the competition of weeds. I must be prepared to work when the sun shines and contend with the weather when it is unfavorable. I must harvest and market my crop prudently. There are some other things, which I can change very little, therefore, I must learn to adapt. To a great extent, this also applies to our lives.

To have a rewarding life, we must decide what crops we are going to raise. Our acreage is vast, so we will plant several crops in our lifetime. Our crops include family, social interests and responsibilities, personal interests, and employment, among others. While the priorities we give to raising these crops is important, it is also important to understand that we will reap a harvest from each one and there is no assurance of a bumper crop. There are always outside factors beyond our control that have great influence on our harvest, and our success with these crops is determined how we manage these uncertainties.

In any case, the formula for raising good crops is the same. We must be sure that we can grow the crop. You don't grow oranges in Alaska and you certainly don't play professional basketball if you are only five feet tall. We must be prudent in our seed selection. We must be sure that our crop is a crop of value and understand that value is not always monetary. In this selection, we must consider our talents, our opportunities, our obligations, along with our dreams.

We must do whatever is necessary to make our fields fertile. This requires study, hard work, and commitment. The world is full of many teachers offering exciting short cuts to bumper crops, and many can show impressive credentials, but the lessons from successful people and proven experiences should be the most honored.

There is always the problem of weed control. These are the little things that can become big things and that keep getting in the way. It could be the company we keep, sometimes it is inattention, and sometimes it is other more glamorous enticements along the way. Good crops need cultivation. This is the effort we must expend to have good friends, happy families, and rewarding vocations. The world really owes you nothing. Even the most basic knowledge indicates that mother earth does not revolve around any one person, you included. We are all fellow passengers on this ride and the trip wasn't planned especially for any one of us. If we expect to be loved, we must be lovable, if we want respect, we must be respectable, if we want help in times of need, we must be helpful, and if we want rewards, we must be productive.

A certain amount of patience is required before there is a harvest. Tiny seeds are planted into the good earth, and for a time they are virtually lost. A combination of good seeds, warm earth, moisture, and a certain miracle beyond our complete understanding will result in a plant emerging. This plant will grow rather slowly and months may pass before there will be a harvest. There are no short cuts, and we dare not overlook the fact that the enjoyment of watching a crop grow provides a value almost as great as the harvest itself. The harvest will come.

If we want to harvest good health, we must eat properly, exercise, avoid contagion, keep busy, and abstain from those harmful chemicals that destroy mind and body. We must remove the notion that a pill or potion will take the place of our inattention and assume the responsibility for our health and safety.

If our harvest is to be social acceptance, it must include honesty and integrity, and for this we must abide by the laws of society and of God, and make amends when we fall short.

Our most valuable earthly crop is a good family. This requires, first, that we are good children, then good parents, and accept an important role in an extended family. We must tend this crop carefully, and be sure to give it enough attention. This crop grows quickly, suffers from competition from all sorts of weeds, and needs constant cultivation, but can give a most bountiful and continuous harvest of both enjoyment and comfort.

We probably plant too many acres to the crop of economics, not so much because of the time consumed raising the crop, but rather because of the actual value of the harvest. It is a glamorous crop that looks good from the road, and because it is such an attractive crop, we plant too much of it and then find out too late that the yield is poor and the market keeps falling. Because we planted so much and the market is poor, we put our crop into storage and then discover that it is a very fragile crop and its value deteriorates rapidly. It is a very useful crop, and that we dare not overlook, but we must not devote acres to it that should be planted to the more valuable crops.

These are all earthly crops and from these we will reap a harvest during our short stay on this good earth, but if there is such a thing as eternity, there is also an eternal harvest. For this harvest, we must give attention in the same way we look after our earthly crops. The "Master Gardener" has provided an instruction manual that not only covers the eternal harvest, but also applies to all of our earthly harvests. All that needs to be said is "When all else fails, read the instructions". Also, it is good to note the warranties that are included.

Supper

I am not sure if dictionary definitions are always correct. Sometimes customs and habits define an event more clearly than a dictionary can. This is true in naming meals. Local culture, family tradition, and even changing times put different meanings to the ritual of eating. Everyone probably understands that the morning meal is breakfast, unless it is late enough to be called brunch. In my experiences, the noon meal was lunch except on Sundays, holidays, or other special occasions, when it was called dinner. I also understand that many people called the evening meal dinner, but down on the farm, our evening meal was called supper, and it was a very special time. The chores of the day would be completed, bits of the good earth would be washed off our hands and faces, the family would all sit down together, and we would be hungry. Usually, this was the biggest meal of the day as well as a time to talk. But there was something more than nutrition that made this meal so important, and so suppertime is probably a better title than just supper. There were certain values experienced at suppertime that were important and hopefully will not be lost in our modern culture.

Supper often included some special food. There were the first spears of asparagus in the spring or those morel mushrooms found in the woods. Later on, there were all sorts of produce from the good earth, which had been patiently coddled from seed to maturity and tenderly prepared by loving hands. There were roasting ears and tomatoes, melons and squash, and berries and fruits picked fresh. There was home grown meat, milk and eggs, and even sometimes some blue gills caught by a young angler. Of course, such food could be bought, but a direct connection between the good earth, loving hands preparing it, and those around the table added a special touch.

Because of this recognized connection, there was always thanks given to a providential God who made such bounty possible. This bounty was recognized as a special blessing, as a result of work, weather, and the miracle of life, rather than a commodity that money could buy. This wholesome food was enjoyed, not because of fancy packaging, endorsement by notable people, or extensive advertising, but rather because we knew where it came from and what it took to produce it.

Suppertime was also a good time to receive instructions in good manners. A complete knowledge of etiquette was not the basis of those instructions, but please and thank you and other common courtesies were demanded. Food would be passed and sometimes choice morsel would even have to be shared and good conversation was encouraged. This was the time when the adventures of the day could be shared, the news of the day discussed, and plans for the future formulated. Often, there were guests. Family, neighbors, children's playmates, and friends just happened to be there at mealtime and share whatever was on the menu for the evening.

This was an informal time when young cooks proudly served their handiwork and some rare failures of experienced cooks or new recipes were served and eaten with something less than enthusiasm. These were the times when children made a mess with their first adventures in the art of eating and there were even some spills from those with more experience, but even if they were viewed at the moment with some exasperation, they soon became laughing matters.

Hunger and malnutrition was unknown, but at times meals might be a bit frugal. Sometimes the budget might be a bit tight, sometimes the menu was "leftovers", and sometimes schedules interfered with a normal meal, but these times were the exceptions, not the rule. In fact, overeating should have been more of a concern than hunger, but a hard day's work made overeating pretty hard to do.

I am sure that it is not a scientific fact, but it seems that food which I have grown has a very special taste. It is not the soil, or the environmental factors that make this difference, but rather some mental and physical conditions that comes with a close association with the good earth. There is the "sweat factor". There is something about the perspiration that adds to the natural flavor of food. This must be family or friend sweat or it has no effect, but it does make food special. There is the "faith factor". Seeds are planted with no guarantee of a good harvest, but somehow, believing that the sun will shine, the rain will fall and the seasons will change, and seeing these things occur, contribute to a sense of security and well being. There is the "patience factor". The production of food takes time and planning. You can not "shop" in a garden on a whim or fancy, but rather needs must be considered and produce harvested in season. There is the "miracle factor". At least to me, a small miracle occurs every time a seed sprouts, grows, and produces a crop. Just because it is so commonplace, does not decrease its qualifications as a miracle. I am not even sure of an exact definition of a miracle, but this amazing process must be so labeled for lack of anything better, and witnessing it first hand does make food taste better.

Suppertime is an almost sacred ritual that seems to be in danger. Ready prepared foods have made the preparation of meals easier, but they also have taken away the need of many of the skills of a good cook and the pride experienced by a good cook. Busy schedules and the availability of fast foods often replace the ritual of sharing a family meal. Special family times need not be suppertime, but there are few substitutes. While pleasant memories do include the food, the most pleasant are reserved for moments spent with those you love. Teasing, sharing family lore, establishing family tradition, soothing broken hearts, laughing together, and even necessary discipline are all part of suppertime.

While there is a certain value to an evening meal concerning good health, the greatest value by far, is the nutrition for the soul, and this value is shared by both those who provide the meal and those who are dependent on it.

The Return To Earth

By all logic, my body will at some time return to the good earth, which has sustained it. Everyone who has experienced life on a farm knows this to be a fact. Farm life includes the start of life, a period of development, a stage of productivity, and the end of life, thus the reality.

On the farm, we knew where our fried chicken and pork chops came from. At some time, we had seen chickens hatch and had watched pigs born, and then watched them grow into a marketable crop. We enjoyed playing with them, helped care for them, and knew of their commercial value. We understood when the weak didn't survive and knew of the loss when accident of disease struck. We helped load chickens and hogs on trucks and watched them go to market, or slaughtered them for our own use, and understood that such was their purpose and destiny.

We also had dogs and cats. These were pets and our relationship with them was much different. They were to be played with and petted and ran free around the farm. They provided companionship and entertainment, but their life spans were much shorter than ours were, and at times we had to bury them and allow them to return to the good earth.

The farm abounded with wildlife. Some were pests, some were edible, and all were interesting to watch and observe. The pests were destroyed whenever possible, and by whatever means were necessary. The deer, rabbits, squirrels, and pheasants were hunted for food and others had values for their pelts, but all were protected by legal means and these laws were respected. We watched these wild creatures, were fascinated by their different ways to survive, and understood that they all had a position on the food chain. It is very rare that these wild creatures return directly to the good earth, Mother Nature is not wasteful.

Dotted here and there around the countryside, are many small cemeteries. Some are well maintained, but many are seemingly forgotten. There are headstones that indicate that at some time, those who are buried there were remembered and well thought of, but time has severed the links to present generations. Most people are indeed foolish to believe that anything different will be their fate. We all will return to the good earth that nurtured and sustained us.

Or will we? From the earliest recorded history, there has always been some sort of belief of a life after an earthly death. In ancient cultures, tombs were filled with all kinds of provisions to ensure a good trip or comfortable existence in an afterlife, all sorts of rites have been observed to get in touch with those departed, and many versions of that great hereafter have been believed. All this and no regular and predictable contact with the departed has ever been established. The wisdom of the ages still seems to believe that in spite of the death of our body, we still live on. I too, am firmly convinced.

I am convinced that there is a Creator God. The world and its containing universe are too well planned and too intricate to be an object of happenstance. There is too much mystery about me and my ability to understand and communicate with my fellow human beings for me to believe that all I am is a physical body. I am convinced that the real me is a soul. While I may believe that there is a definite connection between the soil and the soul, I also believe that the connection ends at my demise and only my body returns to the good earth and my soul claims its just reward. Those country cemeteries contain only markers to indicate that a soul once walked upon this earth.

I do not claim to even vaguely understand the journey of a soul. Somehow, a spark of life gave me being and allowed me an adventure we call life. I know that my humanity allows me a much different existence than the animals I encountered on the farm. All the animals I met were to serve me in one respect or another, and none of them had any capabilities that would have been needed to master me. They could not convey thoughts or ideas with one another or document the past or record the present. They could not add any part of what they might have been taught to anything preceding generation might have been taught and present it to another generation to add to its knowledge or lore. They were not capable of love. They could be faithful, trainable, and even to a degree affectionate, but they lacked the essentials for true love. They could be good instinctive parents, but they had no emotional ties to their parents, siblings, or offspring after the nurturing days were over. Because I could add to the knowledge of others, learn, think, reason, love, and enjoy life rather than just survive, I am convinced I am more than just a body, I am a soul.

Since I am a soul, my connection with the good earth will end, and I will never inhabit a cemetery. My enjoyable adventure on earth will end and I will start another adventure, which will be filled with as many unknowns as this one presented. For this, I must develop a great faith and understand the rules pertaining to my next adventure. The Great Creator, who made my short stay on the good earth so exciting, set the rules for my next adventure and common sense prescribes that I obey them.

My connection with the good earth has been exciting, challenging and rewarding. The feeble glimpse of the intricate workings of this great universe leaves me with great expectations of the knowledge in store as my soul journeys on. Possibly, I will learn the secrets of creating, the boundaries of time and eternity and the other unsolved mysteries of life on our good earth. In any event and whatever adventure awaits my soul, its connection to the good earth has been most enjoyable.

Warning

The second part of this book requires a sort of warning. My contacts with the soil have inspired a lot of "cornfield philosophy" and with this, most people are very comfortable. It can be viewed as quaint colloquialism and passed off with a smile, with the notion that it is just a good lesson in living. It requires no change in attitudes or lifestyle and only suggests a little fine tuning in status quo, but there comes a time when the lessons in life exceed philosophy and become a sort of theology and this is very uncomfortable to many, therefore this warning.

As I have gotten my hands dirty and experienced that close contact with the good earth, mere earthly explanations of the millions of miracles that take place constantly are not enough. I see the hand of a Power that cannot be explained by science or philosophy and a master plan that coincidence will not explain. I have personally experienced the peace and serenity that simple faith provides and view as a terrible waste of time, talent and fortunes the effort spent on research devoted to an unimportant and non-provable ancient past. Aside from curiosity, the value of such studies is only entertainment and has little bearing on the problems of our troubled world or makes any contribution to personal happiness. On the other hand, just the acceptance of a Creator God seems a most logical explanation for all the miracles, which we usually just take for granted, for our existence, and for a definition of any purpose of life.

I would like to offer a theology devoid of details. Details are an individual's opportunity to personalize their faith and could lead to too much controversy rather than focusing on some basic truths. My theology is simple and its presentation is not intended to change or challenge other concepts, gather converts, or denounce other beliefs, but rather present the reasoning behind the faith that has allowed me such peace and serenity.

From all documented history, it is apparent that mankind became a civilized creature at a time roughly corresponding to the account in the Scriptures. Whatever he was before, or even if he was before, there was a time when he started to add knowledge to previous knowledge and to question his purpose in life and his relationship to his Creator. At such a time, acceptable conduct was established, and good and evil was recognized. History reveals that the knowledge that allowed mankind to build great empires also allowed him to do great evil and God sent some simple laws that have been the basis for all civilized behavior. No one has ever disputed that the world would be a much better place if these simple laws were strictly followed, but some inherent weaknesses seem to prevent such obedience. However you want to view Jesus Christ, He did explain those laws and offer a logical solution for a happy life on earth and an eternal reward for those who believe and obey.

The following chapters are based on the Scriptures and are in series of five. They are varied in nature and are intended to provoke your thinking. With all the information available in today's world, it is too easy to depend on the thinking of others and buy into their philosophies and theologies rather than just using their thinking as a stimulant for our own. Our thinking needs guidelines. We need to consider our historical heritage, have a concept of purpose for life, have an idea of the responsibilities that are ours, develop a sense of how we are to relate to our fellow man, and clarify our relationship with God.

My contact with the soil has inspired me to consider my soul. My soul is the real me. It is the part of me that is expressed in thought, reason, adventure, pleasure, excitement, and love. It is what puts us above all other creatures and carries that little portion of God that was shared with us at Eden. It is timeless and its care should take precedence over everything else. It is the key to true happiness.

Charlie Cole

The First Five Questions

Question number one

In considering important issues, I believe it is always a good idea to start at the beginning, which in this case is Eden. Whether or not this was the first appearance of a humanoid on this earth, to me is irrelevant, because I believe that at Eden, the soul was born. It is not even that important that you believed that a snake talked to Eve, or Adam ate that apple. It is however; most important to study some interesting conversations which are recorded in Genesis and which define humanity.

The world was new and undefiled by humanity. The environment and ecosystems were in perfect harmony and working as planned. In the midst of this wonderful creation, God created a being in His own image and provided for him in this place called Eden. In this garden, God could walk with this special creature and share thoughts and emotions. The man could express wonder and awe at the beauty and intricacies of the creation and God could love and pamper His created. It was an ideal situation for both, man was happy and secure and God was proud.

The rules in Eden were very simple. It was man's to use and enjoy, except for the fruit of "The Tree of Knowledge of Good and Evil". This is where the snake came slithering into the picture and asked the first question. It was a simple question and it has been asked many times and in many ways; "If you can eat the fruit of every other tree, why not this one"? The serpent posed the logic that a good God surely would not punish anyone for doing such a simple thing as eating what you were not supposed to eat. The serpent also enticed Eve to believe that this knowledge would make her equivalent to a god. She and Adam did eat and it tasted good and they did learn that there is both good and evil in this world, and the first thing they did with this knowledge was to get dressed.

By any moral consideration, it is hard to understand what could be wrong with knowing good and evil, or what it would be like not to know good and evil. Much of modern thought has trouble defining, acknowledging, and accepting that there is right and wrong, and most of our personal and social ills are a result of this.

The real creation of man was the creation of the spiritual being. God had already made all sorts of animals, so a physical and even mental creation was not new. Animals could exist, grow, reproduce, and had well-developed senses and instincts, but these attributes did not satisfy the Creator. God wanted, and even needed, a creature that could explore and partially understand, and therefore appreciate His marvelous creation. God wanted, and even needed, a being that could share the wonderful emotion of love. God wanted, and even demanded, a being that would worship and recognize Him as creator and provider. God also demanded obedience to His rules, because He knew that such obedience was necessary for mankind's happiness. Such a being would be spiritual and capable of thought, reason and emotion, and would only inhabit a physical body. What Adam and Eve discovered were the senses and the appetites of their physical bodies. This raises the question of whether we are a soul within a body or a body with a soul.

Mankind has struggled with this question ever since and the problem only gets more in evidence when we seem to be more concerned with pampering our bodies and less concerned with the well being of our eternal souls. One of the promises the snake made to Eve was that she would be almost equal to God, Himself, and that notion of power seems to be quite as popular today as it was to her and has been throughout the history of humanity. Because of the great strides in medical science, society is able to take great liberties with birth and death and often seems to regard our earthly existence as our only challenge. Social customs do not encourage the discipline of appetites and then leave so many wondering why they get only increased desires and little satisfaction. Both Adam and Eve found the apple very tasty and forgot to consider the consequences. In today's language, we call it "instant gratification". They had violated the rules but were sure a just and loving God would not punish them for their disobedience.

Poor Eve seems to get all the blame, but over the centuries all of us are still tempted to make the same mistake and the consequences are still the same as when the earth was new. None of us are tempted by talking snakes, our temptations are much more subtle, but each of us face and often fail the same temptations as she did. Pick up a Sunday paper or take note of the commercials on TV and it becomes apparent that someone believes a lot of people are willing to spend much money to maintain, adorn, and pamper their physical bodies. Check the entertainment page and it is apparent that there is a market for some sort of satisfaction for physical senses and appetites. Often, all this at the expense of acknowledging we are really a soul. Adam and Eve threw away a very good deal and except for the fact that God was proud of, and loved His creation, we would never have had the pleasure of our existence.

The snake still asks the same question; "Would a loving God punish you for eating just one apple"? Evidently, the answer was yes, and still is, unless we accept His plan for forgiveness.

Adam and Eve learned that there is good and evil. The good is that we do have appetites, which we are to use and enjoy, and the evil enters in when these appetites are not controlled, and this is not an easy challenge. And do we believe ourselves to be a lesser god? All too often we take the word of the snake and believe that we can be, and in so doing, miss the harmony with God our father Adam once enjoyed. It would do us well to discover who we really are; an eternal soul created as only an image of God, our Creator.

The Second Question

It must have been a very lovely day in Eden. The sun had gone down and God was walking in His garden. He wanted to walk and have a little talk with His very special creation, so He called out; "Where are you"? Adam answered that he had been hiding because he didn't have any clothes on and was ashamed of his nakedness. God's next question was; "When did you realize you were naked and did you eat fruit from that forbidden tree"? Adam confessed, blamed Eve, and Eve blamed the snake.

Eden has the reputation of being the ideal place, but I wonder about running around wearing no clothing. It would have to be an ideal climate, which would require no protection, and surely branches would scratch and bugs would bite.

When God had to call Adam, it raised three questions, which are legitimate today. Do we still try to run and hide from God, why are we wearing clothes, and do we still try to "pass the buck"?

We may not have quite as close a relationship with God as Adam enjoyed, but He would still like to walk and talk with us. We will probably not hear a voice from heaven or a burning bush, or from some sacred or hallowed spot, but He would still like to talk to us. Sometimes we can listen with our eyes and hear Him in the wonders of the universe, sometimes in kind words from others, and other times it is that "still small voice" from deep within our conscience. Too often, we are too busy to listen or want to do all the talking, but once in a while when He speaks and we hear and we still try to hide.

We get embarrassed if we think we are naked in the presence of God, but the truth is, we are more than unclothed. Our very thoughts and emotions are in full view of God and we are no more successful in our hiding than Adam was.

God asked Adam how he knew he was naked, or; "Why are you wearing that fig leaf apron"? I know several very good reasons why I wear clothing. Anyone living in my area in January has a very good reason to wear lots of clothing, and in the heat of summer the medical profession warns against too much direct sunlight on bare skin. I also look much better in clothing; clothing covers many bulges, wrinkles, and other imperfections. I also must confess, as a descendent of Adam, I must contend with the knowledge of good and evil and I would have trouble keeping only pure thoughts if all those around me were unclothed. Possibly, I am not alone in my reasons for wearing clothes, and possibly, others wear clothing for much the same reasons.

God then asked Adam if he had eaten any apples, and some other "human nature" came forth. The art of "passing the buck" was born, and in our present day of "enlightenment", we have developed this art almost to perfection. In the simple time of Eden, there were few culprits to blame for any transgressions. Eve took the first hit and she passed it right on to the snake. Today, we are much more sophisticated. We can blame heredity, the rest of society; lack of opportunity, diet, or any number of things and the list tends to grow almost daily.

In this story of Adam and Eve, mankind had lost its innocence and thereby some of its close relationship with God. Mankind was no longer just a spiritual being, but also recognized that he was also a physical creature with all the lusts a physical body would impose on him. Mankind could be a victim of its appetites, that fruit was tasty, and the lure of power came into existence, the snake promised that Adam and Eve could become like a god. It is hard to imagine what kind of power Adam and Eve could have wanted, since God had provided so well for them, but the notion of not having to obey any higher power took root. They also noted that they were naked, so they made aprons to cover their bodies. They tried to hide and escape reality. They offered excuses and tried to blame their sin on someone else. Today, we like to call these things "natural" and accept them as just part of life, but we must remember that it was not intended to be that way, or had to be that way, and there was a short time when such weaknesses were not a way of life.

Surely, Adam's sin saddened God. He wanted His special creation to remain innocent and walk in the garden with Him and talk to Him, but this could no longer be. Like a parent with a much loved, but disobedient child, God had to punish these creatures He loved so much, for that act of disobedience. Adam and Eve got kicked out of Eden and had to go to work. They had to experience pain, sorrow, and fear, and they had to hoe the weeds out of their garden. That heritage has been passed to each of us.

That has been the story of mankind as a whole, possibly you, and definitely me. Instead of a nice walk with God and the warmth of a loving conversation with Him, I often am tempted to try to hide, I can find excuses rather than offer apologies and ask forgiveness, and I know that I break God's heart and He has reason to punish me. I am a failure since I have never have lived up to the expectations our Creator had for me. But He still loves me, in fact, so much, that He sent His Son to redeem me from the sin of discovering I am a physical being and forgetting I am an eternal soul.

Question Number Three

Mankind had lost his innocence and was now capable of evil thoughts and therefore evil deeds. The next question God asks is very interesting. We do not know to whom God directs the question, but He asks; "What if man eats from the Tree of Life and lives forever"? God recognized that man had learned of his physical desires, that is, good and evil and was concerned that he might eat from the Tree of Life and have an eternal existence on earth. In fact, God was so concerned about this that He banished him forever from Eden and even placed mighty angels with flaming swords to keep man from ever entering the garden and eating from the Tree of Life. What danger could this Tree of Life pose and what could be the consequences that would be so serious that God had to post a guard so Adam couldn't even get near that tree? What could God mean when He expressed the fear that man might live forever?

In our perspective, Adam seemed to come close to living forever. He lived 930 years. If Adam had died yesterday, he would have been a Knight with the crusaders while he was in his thirty's. He would have been about 425 years old if he would have wanted to sail with Columbus. He would have been about 550 years if had sailed on the Mayflower, and he would have been over 700 years old if he had signed the Declaration of Independence. God granted him a very long life span, but yet feared some secret learned from the Tree of Life would pose a threat to God himself or to His creation.

This knowledge must be very dangerous and, personally, I don't care to know this secret, but it does raise some questions as to man's quest for knowledge. Knowledge begets knowledge and with the development of the computer, knowledge grows with leaps and bounds. In our lifetime, we have seen the secret of the atom discovered and the destruction of civilization within the reach and control of mankind. We have seen our lifetime expand to the point that within the foreseeable future, it will pose serious social and economic problems. We have consumed so much energy that, if not us, our children or grandchildren will have to find some alternative to fossil fuel. We generate mountains of waste, of which, some is quite hazardous and have not found ways of sensibly disposing it. We bring into the world some who should not live and keep alive some who should die and have not solved the moral consequences of either. We have explored the mind and with that understanding, seem to only cause more confusion and problems rather than solving them. We have an Internet that puts all manner of information at the fingertips of everyone and are only beginning to see the problems related to it. To simplify, our knowledge has far outdistanced our wisdom in using it.

With all this knowledge, what could it be that we don't know? There seems to be only two dimensions we haven't breached, how to create and how to control time. We still cannot make something from nothing, destroy anything, or start a life process, and only in science fiction, has the time machine been invented. Whether or not these concepts were contained in that Tree of Life is only a guess, but with mankind's track record with other scientific achievements, God had better guard these dimensions with a flaming sword.

Suppose Adam had eaten from that tree and mankind would never have to face death. Of course, the world would be getting a little crowded by now, and that would be a big problem. Understanding evil and knowing that there was no death, what kind of society would mankind have developed? Death is the ultimate punishment, whether it is worldly punishment or eternal destiny. It is quite evident that God did not want anybody to live on earth eternally.

We have ended up with a much better deal than Adam. He only lived 930 years and we all expect to live eternally. Could this Tree of Life have been God's plan of salvation and only guarded because it was not time for it to be revealed? Without the fear of death, would mankind who knew both good and evil, do only good? Would the promise of heaven and no threat of Hell cause any of us to do only good? We like to believe that we are only motivated to do good because of love, but in all honesty, the threat of eternal punishment probably motivates all of us to some degree. It becomes understandable why God guarded that tree so well. Knowing evil makes all of us imperfect and until an eternal home was prepared by Jesus Christ, death was a certainty for each of us.

We know that God loved His innocent creation and was disappointed when that innocence was lost. We can also be sure that God does not want His eternal home contaminated by mankind who had lost that innocence any more than He wanted Eden occupied by imperfect people. This home was not to be occupied by a bunch of sinners, and we are all sinners until we accept the atonement offered by the death and resurrection of Jesus Christ. Adam was kicked out of paradise because of sin, but all of us, in spite of our sins, are welcome in paradise if we only believe. How could we ask for more?

Question Four

Adam and Eve were kicked out of the Garden of Eden and had to go to work. Weeds started to grow in their gardens and they suffered pain and fear such as we all experience. In the course of time, they had two sons, Cain and Abel, and of course, they had to earn a living too. Cain was what we would call a dirt farmer and Abel was a sheepherder. It is very interesting to note that both these boys understood the concept of stewardship. It is evident that God still kept very close contact with His favorite creation, and although mankind had learned good and evil, he still recognized, worshipped and had close contact with God. Even though it was not Eden anymore, the world was, and still is, a wonderful piece of craftsmanship. While not perfect, life was, and still is, good.

Somehow, Cain and Abel both recognized the necessity of bringing an offering to God. There is no record of God requiring such an offering, but each did present to God a portion of his produce. Cain had brought some of that produce, but the record states that Abel brought the best of his flock, inferring that Cain's offering was of lesser quality or possibly something that was left over or not needed. God was very happy with Abel's offering, but was very disappointed with Cain's, and Cain got very angry. God noted this and asked; "Why are you angry"?

This is the first recorded lesson in stewardship, and the lesson taught is that why we give is more important than how much we give. The Scriptures give much attention to wealth and the use of it, so it must be a serious spiritual problem. Our problem with wealth begins with failing to recognize that we own nothing and that helping others is more of a blessing to the giver than the receiver.

God went on to patiently explain to Cain that if he had done well, there would be no reason to be angry, and that such anger could get him in a lot of trouble. God saw a human weakness cropping out. Instead of recognizing his mistake and attempting to correct it, apologizing to God for doing less than expected or even blaming God for asking too much, Cain blamed his brother. Could it be that any of us might have inherited just a bit of this weakness from our ancient ancestors?

I must confess that at times I do get a bit angry and have noted that most of the people who I come in contact with also get angry at times, and God still asks us why we are angry and warns us that anger will get us in a lot of trouble. We see the results of anger all around us. Scan any newspaper on any day and note the results of anger. There are murders, wars, broken families, and subtle signs of unhappiness that make headlines, and there are untold numbers of broken hearts and ruined relationships that prevent people from enjoying life to the fullest. We overlook the notion that God wants us to be happy and all His instructions for living are for our benefit, not to put a rein on our freedom. The question remains; "Why are we angry"? Is it because we believe the world revolves around us rather than recognizing that we are only passengers for a short ride? Could it be that we think that those around us are there for our use only? Could it be that it is so handy to blame our faults and weaknesses on someone else?

Whatever our excuse for being angry, it still will get us in a lot of trouble. It can be our greatest stumbling block to our personal happiness. Most of our anger is caused by taking little things too seriously and allowing little irritations to grow into big problems. We must also understand that others do not make us angry, we make ourselves angry. It is not what happens, but rather how we react to an event or a person, and if it is our problem, the cure is also ours.

The world is no longer Eden and since Adam and Eve made a mistake, neither us nor the people around us are perfect. This we must recognize if we are to live happily in the world around us.

The Fifth Question

Cain was very jealous. His kid brother had done something better than he had. Both of them had done something good, but one had done something better. Cain should have learned a valuable lesson. God had not severely punished him for offering a lesser gift, only reprimanded him, and all he would have to have done was to bring a proper gift the next time. He could have apologized to God and even had the opportunity to invent the phrase "I didn't know". He could have used that mistake as a learning experience and God would have no doubt been pleased. But that didn't happen.

He had learned from his mother and father to blame someone else, so he took out his anger on his brother. I am aware how such things get started and can visualize what probably happened. The Scriptures state that the boys were in the fields, they talked, and soon Cain got so angry he killed his brother. They probably started by talking about crops and sheep, the conversation got around to their offerings, they started yelling at each other, did a little pushing and shoving, and finally, Abel got killed. Today, we would call it second degree murder.

From this fight, came two questions. First, God simply asked where He could find Abel, and Cain lied and said he didn't know. The next question was asked by Cain, and is often quoted even today, when he asked God; "Am I my brother's keeper "?

Lying to anyone who knows the truth is always very stupid and dangerous, and this is especially true when dealing with God. Amongst us earthly dwellers, there is possibly a little leeway concerning the absolute truth. We don't always tell others how they look or how we feel, we call it tact. It would be quite a disservice to tell someone he was ugly, and no one really wants to know all the details when we feel poorly. It would be of no use to tell our children all our past mistakes or burden them with the everyday problems of providing for their well being. We have labeled some of these things "white lies".

Not being honest with God is another matter. It is interesting to note that "excuses" evidently had not been invented yet, at least Cain didn't use one. In our modern culture, since we know about "excuses", we would have called it an accident, or it just slipped, or he hit me first, or I didn't mean it, and we definitely would call a lawyer. We can get very comfortable with our sins and in our times of "enlightenment", and we seem to have all kinds of legitimate reasons for our trespasses, and all too often we even take refuge behind that Amazing Grace rather than correcting our flaws.

Then Cain asked his famous question. It is interesting to note that God didn't say yes or no, and so the question remains today. Jesus Christ answered the question of who are brother is and made it clear we are to help others when necessary, but are we our brother's keeper?

One of the great blessings of our creation is our individuality. Whether we talk about fingerprints or personalities, we are all different. We are not predestined clones or robots, but very unique individuals. We all make conscious decisions concerning everything we do or say and each one of us has made some poor decisions. Each of us, at some time or another, has needed help from those around us, either because of those poor decisions or from what we like to call bad luck. Some of those poor decisions had little or no serious consequences, others caused much trouble, but in every case, they became a portion of our lives. We also have made many good decisions, and with these we do not hesitate to take credit. Who we are is a result of our decisions and our reaction to the situations we encounter in our lives.

While we should never be so smug with ourselves that we can see no need for improvement, or so weak we will not try to improve ourselves. We must recognize that, for the most part, we have made ourselves who we are, and few of us would be willing to give up that choice. Being my brother's keeper implies that I will be making choices for him that I believe will affect his well being, and if I make those choices for him, then I must allow my brother to make such choices for me. If I am to keep my brother, then I must be willing to assume the responsibility of the results of my influence and if he keeps me, I must live with the results of his influence. While we were created to be close social beings, we were also given the responsibility for our own lives.

Cain just changed the subject. God didn't expect him to take care of his brother; Abel was perfectly capable of taking care of his own sheep. Neither did God expect him to do his brother any harm. God didn't ask Cain if he had neglected his brother or even if he had been fighting with him, just where he was, and Cain lied and tried to change the subject.

Today we hear the same question and often it is asked in the same light as when Cain asked it. Jesus Christ made it pretty clear who our brother is but we struggle to understand if we are to be his keeper or even what it means to be his keeper. There is no doubt that we are not to intentionally harm those around us. There is no doubt that we are to help others when they need help. There is also little doubt God expects us to be responsible individuals, but there is a great question as to when help destroys another's individuality. God did not answer Cain because the question was not pertinent to the situation.

Are we our brother's keeper? Adversary, definitely not; helper, remember the story of the Good Samaritan; keeper, not if it destroys his individuality and often we find hard to understand the difference between helping and keeping.

Charlie Cole

The House

The center of every farm is the homestead. This is where the barns, outbuildings, and homes are located. This is where you will find lawns, flowers, and gardens and is the true center of living for those who love the land. This center requires a lot of upkeep. Buildings need constant repair and maintenance, lawns must be mowed, and gardens planted. A certain amount of knowledge of carpentry and construction is a vital part of life down on the farm.

My neighbor once had a bumper sticker that read; "My Boss is a Jewish Carpenter", and I also claim the Jewish Carpenter as my boss. In His time, carpentry was quite different than it is today. In His day, there were no power tools or convenient lumberyards, so it required hard physical labor with very primitive tools and much skill. He did not build houses, but rather hand crafted tools and furniture. Houses were built of stone and masonry, but from His teachings, it is evident that He was familiar with the construction of houses and He used that knowledge as examples for living. Much of His mission was to issue instruction for building lives, not only for new lives, but also instructions for repairing and remodeling older lives.

The Site

The first requisite for a house is a place to put it and in this respect, we have inherited a wonderful building site. God has provided us with a world that provides beauty, convenient utilities, and pleasant surroundings. All around us is beauty, and we, as a creation in the image of God, are the only creatures that can see this beauty. We can see color, proportion and harmony and we should be thankful, not only for this beauty, but also for the ability to translate it into an enjoyable sensation. Our world is also a marvelously functioning mechanism. As it spins and orbits, the functions that govern its physical nature are exact and measurable, and we can use these laws for our comfort and convenience. Our world is filled with people. These people come in all sizes, shapes, and colors, and can provide comfort, joy, and love if we allow it.

Take a look at the world around us. The hills and valleys hint at the vastness of this world, and the flowers and sky provide a spectrum of color. As we look at a tree, we should be amazed at the process that transforms air, water, a few minerals, and sunlight into something so majestic and useful. When we look at animal life, whether it is a beast or a bug, we should understand the necessity for balance of all these creatures and how we are to fit into it. A look at fields of grain should make us feel thankful for abundance and surpluses rather than shortages and appreciate the many tasty ways the nutrition for our bodies can be prepared. A look at the rivers and streams should cause us to marvel at the cycle that feeds them and their usefulness. Looking at the sky allows us to read the clues for upcoming weather; the blue assures us of the warmth of sunshine and the clouds assure us of needed rain. When we talk with that friend, hug that child, or share with our spouse, we can savor the best things in life. The sky is also a window for us to see displays of tremendous power and energy, and we must be aware of the potential dangers of lightening, wind and rain. Under us are the rocks and minerals which provide our metals and fuel, and the soil which can be tilled to provide our food and fiber.

This is a most wonderfully planned creation and on this site we are to build our lives. With every building site there is a cost, and with us, the deal is unique. Our site is not for sale and cannot be bought but rather a conditional lease. We are to appreciate it, try to understand it, use it, care for it, and understand the concept of stewardship. This may seem a small price for our tenancy, but far too often, we fail to pay even this small price. The legacy of humankind has been to regard this good earth as his possession and to fight over portions of it, abuse it, destroy it, and waste its bounty. We take the beauty for granted and only appreciate it when it is gone, and pollute the air, water, and soil and pass it off as the price for progress. We interrupt the balance of nature rather than work with it, and fail miserably at learning and practicing stewardship.

Any power lesser than a loving and forgiving God would have imposed sun, water, and air taxes and, with the threat of turning off these utilities, any of us would gladly pay any price asked. But that is not the way it is. This site was prepared especially for us and God was proud of His handiwork. Would it be asking too much for us to stop occasionally and look up, down and around and express appreciation for the beauty around us? Couldn't we conserve, protect, and recognize that we are part of the environment and be better stewards of this good earth?

This seems to be a very small price for our wonderful building site.

The Foundation

We have a beautiful building site; the next step is constructing a good foundation. A good foundation involves more than meets the eye. It is the base on which the rest of the structure is built. A good foundation must be straight, square and level. It must contain quality and long lasting materials and must not be affected by the elements.

Some time ago, I had the "privilege" to put in a foundation for a small addition to a house. It was one of those personal contacts with the good earth with a pick and shovel. Our sub-soil is very hard clay and would appear to make a very firm foundation, but the building code required a depth of thirty-six inches to get below the frost line. The construction of commercial buildings requires more massive foundations and the tallest of buildings often are anchored into bedrock. The lack of a good solid base often limits the possible height of a building. My "Carpenter Boss" was aware of this when He talked about houses being built on rock rather than sand.

Aside from being strong, straight, and level, a foundation is the connection of the building to something solid and unmovable, and no matter how good it looks, how level it is, or how strong it is, it must set on something that will not move, sink, or deteriorate. Good lives must be built on similar qualities. The world around us offers many attractive, strong, and level foundations that often do not go deep enough to set on something unmovable.

We are citizens of the greatest nation on earth. It provides justice, protection, and opportunity as no nation ever has, and we rightly rely on this. But governments are powerful and they, by force or enticement, present themselves as answers to many problems. Governments are merely extensions of powerful people and the lust and greed of these people is often reflected in the role government demands. In our case, we have a voice in government and therefore a duty to see that our government is based on something more solid and unmovable than power and greed. There may be a few small cracks in our government's foundation and these should be repaired as needed, but even with repairs, the best of governments are not the best foundations for life. Our lives must be based on something more solid. Our ethics, morals, manners and actions must be based on something deeper than prescribed by governments and their laws.

We pride ourselves in our affluence. We so often subscribe to the notion that wealth is the yardstick of success. Ease, luxury, and security are too often regarded as the ultimate goals in life, and this quest is the basis for our education, the consumer of out time, and the object of our energy. While slothfulness and laziness are sins, the pursuit of wealth is a pursuit of a very temporary foundation. Instead of the only foundation for life, it should be viewed as just an important block or stone in the foundation, and how wealth is acquired, how it is used, and how it is regarded, determines its value in building a life.

We stress education, but this can be a very dangerous foundation. Too often this foundation is too shallow and is only set on whims and fancies of the times and the wisdom that has been proven as true over the ages is ignored. Technology seems to bring out conceit and our morality fails to deal with the impact of our discoveries. We edit history rather than learn from it, and the arts assume the role of teacher rather than entertainer. We also overlook the fact that we all get educated, whether it is from experience, society around us, or in a formal way. This is the reason education must be built on the facts my "Carpenter Boss" presented. If these facts are not firmly in place, they will be replaced with material that will crumble when tested by time.

We also like to build on religion. Mere ritual, social involvement, and emotional outlet often crowd out true faith. The rock my "Boss" referred to was not a religion, but rather a faith based on love, commitment, atonement, and forgiveness.

Building a foundation is hard work whether it be for a small addition to a house, or for a life. Once it is in, it is almost impossible to tear out and repairs are costly. This makes it very important to set them on something solid below the frost line, use good material, and make them level and straight. Failure to do that will result in a life that will lean; sag, shake, and even eventually fall. A very poor foundation can look very good for a while, but will fail miserably over time. Foundations, for the most part are unseen and lie deep underground and any weaknesses that are built into them is not apparent until tested by storm. This makes it more important than ever to build well. We have a very good blueprint and it is our responsibility to follow this print and if it is followed, we have an unconditional warranty that is good for eternity.

The Walls

We have our site, and a good foundation. The next step is the walls and this is a very important part of this construction. Could you imagine a house without walls? In winter, they keep the snow from drifting in your living room, and in summer they keep out the flies, mosquitoes, and the neighbor's dog and kids. They also, to a certain extent, keep out those who would steal from you or molest you. They also give you privacy and are considered quite essential, especially around bathrooms and bedrooms. As we construct these walls, we will put in windows. Sometimes, windows are used for ventilation, but in this day and age, are primarily used to see what is happening outside. Of course, if we can see out, others can see in, so we cover our windows with drapes, curtains and blinds so we can have control over our privacy. We also put doors in our walls.

Through these openings we come and go, and allow to enter, those we wish to visit or to do business with. The purpose of walls is protection and privacy.

When we build lives, we also must put up walls and sometimes this goes a bit contrary to modern thought. The fact is we are in this adventure of life alone. Even if we have all kinds of support from family and friends, we, and we alone, are responsible for our thoughts and actions. We are individuals, each with a mind and a mind unique. Our personality, our morality, and our success or failure is all determined by how we train and use our minds. Because of these factors, our minds are very private. In this privacy, come all kinds of thoughts, some enlightening, some useful, some worth sharing, and some so private we dare not share them with anyone. There are many things that influence our thoughts. There is childhood training, formal education, lifetime experiences, ambition, challenges, and association with family and friends. There are also negative thoughts that we acquired from our father, Adam, such as greed, hate, lust, and apathy, and we must contend with them regularly. Of course, there are all kinds of help with this conflict, but ultimately, our decisions are ours and ours alone. While we are building our lives, we must recognize that we are very private individuals. No one can teach us until we want to learn, those around us cannot force us to sin, and we do well only by conscious effort.

Although we are private, we must put in windows, there is a world out there and we must be aware of it even when we don't always like what we see. We can put a big picture window in our house so we can see the fields and woods and then have someone tear up the fields, or destroy the woods. In their place put in a highway, build a factory, or operate a landfill and all we can do is pull the drapes. We must be prepared, when circumstances change, friends fail, or the storms of life rage, to pull the drapes. On the other hand, we must also open the drapes and let the sunshine in, open the window and air out the house, and look out and watch the children at play. While we like the privacy of our bathroom, we also like to open the drapes to show off the parlor, so we put a very small window in our bathroom and the living room has a picture window. In building lives, we must be sure we take this into consideration.

Our lives must have doors. This allows others to come into our lives and us to enter theirs. We control this door. We can keep the unwanted salesman from getting his foot in the door and we can invite friends to come in and visit, and we can leave through these doors and visit others.

Sometimes we do pretty stupid things with our walls. Sometimes we get concerned with little things that annoy us and overlook the big things that can hurt us, or we try to keep out the flies and mosquitoes and leave the door wide open. Sometimes we ignore a problem and instead of resolving it, we just pull the drapes and hope the scene changes.

Most important of all, my "Carpenter Boss" will be on your doorstep wanting to come in and help. My boss, being a carpenter, can do much more than just talk. He can move windows and change the view. If that landfill ruined the view from your picture window, He can put that window on the other side of the house. He can replace that torn screen that allows all those pesky bugs to get in. He can even build a new addition that will give you more room and a better view, or any other repairs or improvements your house may need. While most contractors prefer new construction, He specializes in remodeling and repair, and the price is always right. This price was paid a long time ago and there is an eternal guarantee on His work. You don't even have to call Him, because He is always standing at your door whenever you need Him. If you don't let Him in, you are missing the deal of a lifetime.

The Roof

We have our beautiful building site, have a good foundation, and the walls are in place, now we need a roof. The most important function of a roof is to keep out the rain and sun, especially the rain. An abandoned house will stand pretty well until the roof starts to leak, then the timbers will start to rot, and it will eventually fall down. Even small leaks in occupied houses will damage the interior and need immediate attention. To have a good house, the rains must be kept out. This does not mean that rain is a bad thing, but the same rain that makes the lawn green and the roses bloom can ruin your house unless it has a good roof.

In building lives, we also need protection from good things. We are constantly warned about bad and evil things, but are seldom warned about good things, when in fact, we are probably better able to handle diversity than prosperity. A look at history should point this out. Adam and Eve had it made in Eden, but they couldn't handle it, and we have been paying for it ever since. The Children of Israel were given the Promised Land and in several generations it became a world power, but they squandered it, and today David and Solomon's empire is no more than a small troubled nation. Rome ruled the world and was unconquerable, but fell apart at the seams from internal problems, and even our great nation should see some warning flags flying. The same is true of individuals. Take a look at the entertainment and athletic heroes, and note their addictions, heartbreaks and even suicides. Take a look at your friends and neighbors and probably some of them were a lot nicer when they were still struggling. It should be apparent that people often have trouble with good things.

The Scriptures record a visit of a rich young kid to my "Carpenter Boss". You can read about it in Matthew 19, Mark 10, or Luke 18, note that it was recorded three times, so it must be important. This kid thought he was a pretty good guy because he knew all rules and laws and obeyed them. My Boss agreed that he was a real nice fellow and only needed one slight correction, he had to get rid of the good things and give them to those less fortunate. This wasn't what the kid wanted to hear. He probably wanted a pat on the back, but instead, my boss saw a flaw and pointed it out. The problem wasn't the poverty of others, but rather, a good person's wealth. The kid said he had followed the law, therefore he had given generously to the church, but that wasn't enough, so he went away unhappy. My boss saw that the rich kid's wealth was the most important thing in his life, and to give it up was just too much to ask. The kid had a good building site, he was a descendant of Abraham, he had an excellent foundation, he knew the law and followed it, his walls had windows and doors, he let my boss in to visit, but his roof leaked and he wouldn't fix it. That kid probably thought my boss would look at his house and admire his lawn and garden, praise him for having a deep, straight and solid foundation, and comment on the view from his living room, but instead, he saw some loose shingles.

Sometimes, leaky roofs are hard to fix. The water will leak in and run down a rafter and cause damage some distance from the problem. This kid had such a problem. His whole roof didn't blow off; he had some damage away from the leak. It wasn't all that money; it was what he thought about that money. It wasn't the kid's dollars, they could do a lot of good, but that those good dollars had became a sort of god to him.

Few of us are as affluent as that rich kid, but in building our life, we must be sure that our roof will protect us from some of those good things we all strive for. We work hard and want to acquire a certain degree of wealth. We like to be well thought of by our friends and neighbors and we like a little ease and comfort, even a little luxury. We like a little influence and clout, and these are all good things. When we earn more, we can give more, when we are well thought of, we can share happiness, when we have ease and comfort, we will have more time to help others, and with influence, we can become role models. On the other hand, wealth can make us greedy, our popularity make us vulnerable to peer pressure, ease and comfort can make us lazy and irresponsible, and influence can lead to a lust for power.

Sorting out the good things is very hard to do. We do need water in our house, but lets make sure it comes in through the pipes where we have a handle on the faucet, rather than a hole in the roof.

The Decorations

Our house is now well built, but there is something lacking, and the void must be filled before our house will show its full value. There are three things that can detract from the full value of even the finest houses and they must be corrected. The first is emptiness. When was the last time you saw an empty house? When the professionals want to show a house, promote a new addition, or have a parade of homes, they make sure their houses are well furnished and attractively decorated. Next, is a dirty house. This is not about a misplaced magazine, a coffee cup on the table, or even furniture that is showing a little wear, but rather accumulated filth. The third problem is the other side of the coin, a house that is so elegant and so well kept that a person cannot feel comfortable in it. Houses have to be lived in to be made into a home and these homes reflect our likes and dislikes and are a true reflection of ourselves.

So it is with building our lives. Like an empty house, we can live an empty life. Life is supposed to be more than a mere existence, it is an adventure. No one has ever completely planned his life, but rather has formed his life as he has reacted to different situations, surmounted obstacles that got in the way, and took advantage of opportunities as they have occurred. During this adventure, we have experienced excitement; remember the first date or the first kiss, or the first paycheck, or the big game, or the birth of your children, or that close call? During this adventure we have worked hard; remember how hard we had to study for that important test, or the extra hours spent to get an important job done, or getting up in the middle of the night to comfort a crying child? We all have faced obstacles; remember the deal that fell through, or the job that disappeared, or the health problems, or the people around that failed? We have even faced tragedies; remember the business venture that failed, or that broken heart, or the passing of a loved one? These are the things which fill our lives.

Like the too elegant house, we can try to make our lives too sterile. We can put our head in the sand and ignore what is happening in the world around us, when the truth is that there is a real world out there and we must do all we can to improve it. Our neighbor with his soiled shoes can not be turned away just to keep the carpet clean. It would be so nice if we could impose good manners, high morals, and our religion on those around us, but we can't. We know how to make the world better, but it just won't listen.

We can preach, teach, and even set a pretty good example, but the world just seems to look the other way until there is trouble, and then it comes knocking on our door and we must let them in, dirty shoes and all.

Our lives can get a little dirty. We seem to track in some grass after we mow, pick up a little mud after it rains, or leave a little puddle when the snow melts off our shoes. We know there will always be laundry and dirty dishes, and dust and cobwebs seem to come from nowhere. We know we make little messes in our lives and have to wipe them up, but also, there always seems to be a little dirt that pops up out of nowhere. We are a little unkind, just don't like someone, have a prejudice or fail to help our neighbor. Even clean houses need cleaned.

My "Carpenter Boss", not only builds good houses, but also runs a very good cleaning and decorating service. He knows how to take drabness out of a house. He prescribes love.

He knows that love will also be the motivator to keep the house in good order and it will give it the warmth and comfort, which will attract others. He also knows what to throw out of the drawers and closets and what to keep. We all accumulate junk and outgrow or wear out clothes. We fill our closets with things bought on the spur of the moment and hate to throw out. We have shelves full of stuff that keeps us from finding the things we need. He will make your house orderly. He will also get rid of the dirt. We tend to just sweep it under the carpet; He gets rid of it. He will lift up the sofa cushions and clean up the popcorn and dropped crumbs, the leftovers from something good. He will polish the floors and strangers will have a good first impression. He will even make the beds and do the dishes if we allow Him to come often enough. He will provide a doormat that says welcome and allow you to wipe the filth of the world from your feet before you track it into your house. And for all this, what is the cost? It has all been paid. What a deal!

Five Hills

There is something fascinating about hills and mountains. From the bottom, looking up, they present certain grandeur, or they appear as a challenge, either to climb or bypass, and from the top, they present a panorama of all the surrounding territory. In my travels, I have often pulled onto designated areas to note a particular spectacular view of a valley below. On my farm, I have a hill. It is really a very small hill and part of a cultivated field, but from the top, I can see almost every corner of my farm and it is a joy and inspiration to look over the fields and watch crops in their different stages of growth. There is something inspiring from a view from a hill. I am going to relate five tales concerning hills and mountains. Some parts of these stories may be hard to believe, but allow me a little leeway with absolute and proven facts, and search for some truths rather than focusing on possible fiction.

Ararat

Over the past several years, there has been a book written and even a movie produced concerning some discoveries in the Ararat Mountains of what appears to be the remains of Noah's Ark. These mountains lie between Turkey and Russia and some of the peaks reach 17000 feet. The claim is that the ark grounded about 14000 and has been preserved in the ice and snow and, periodically, becomes visible as the snowfield shifts. The site is virtually inaccessible, but has been known by those native to the region for many years. Verification and exploration has been almost impossible because of political reasons, but on several occasions, those native to the region have gained access to what is believed to be the ark and have returned with scraps of wood to verify its existence. Recently, some of these scraps of wood have been examined, and on them, some interesting writings have been discovered that have corresponded to some other ancient writings found carved in stone in a valley of those mountains. With the addition of the writings found on those scraps of wood, the scholars have been able to crack the code and decipher both the wood and the stone. This is the story from the wood and the stone.

The ancient writings seem to be a kind of diary and they are signed; Shem, the son of Noah. The first entry tells of the terrible conditions in the world before the great flood. He tells of the inter-marrying of the descendents of Adam and the other humanoids that inhabited the world and their lack of any conscience, moral restraint, or the ability for love or commitment. This hybrid was capable of reason and thought, but lacked the self-control and conscience that God expected of those created in His image. The result was moral anarchy and complete chaos and it was evident that something had to be done.

Shem writes; "God's instructions to my father seemed very strange, He had instructed him to build this strange and gargantuan structure. This thing was tremendous in size, was to be able to float, and contained numberless pens and stalls. It is impossible to describe the work involved in felling trees, hauling logs, hewing timbers and erecting this structure, and the jeering of those who saw that thing being built on dry land. Understand that my father was over 500 years old at this time and had during his lifetime amassed great wealth and was able to hire much help. This was especially useful in rounding up, capturing, or buying the animals and necessary provisions for those who were supposed to inhabit that huge structure. The help we hired was eager to get the wages and the threat of destruction meant nothing to them as long as they could afford the pleasures of the moment. And then the rains came"

Another entry reads; "It is difficult to describe life on that ark. It is dark and dreary and the smell is stifling. The cleaning, watering, and feeding takes every waking moment and the mooing, roaring, barking, howling, screaming, and hooting is deafening".

The next entry reads; "We have been shut up in this stinking old ark with all this noise, and with all this smell for fifteen and a half months. A few days ago, I was deep inside the ark feeding the elephants. It is hard to imagine how much an elephant can eat until you actually have to feed one. I was tired of the whole situation and in poor spirits, when my father called and asked me to witness some strange color in the sky. I was in no mood to be bothered, and I missed the first rainbow".

This is Shem's last entry on the scraps of wood; "The water has finally gone down and the ground has finally dried up. The world has a sweet freshness and it is good to once again breathe that fresh air. I must admit that I, at times, am a bit surly from the many months of confinement and hard labor and my first comments were; "How are we ever going to get down off this mountain"? The air was cold and we were sitting on rocks high above the green valleys below, and a journey to those green valleys seemed almost as hard as the rest of the adventure. We will start tomorrow".

The rest of the story comes from the inscribed stone. It too is signed "Shem, the son of Noah".

"The world is such a beautiful place. It now teems with life and is so serene and peaceful. I now have time to reflect on the adventure in the ark and want to preserve these reflections in stone so all future generations will know what I have learned.

God does provide. He gives us the instructions to build arks, points to the forests, and gives us the strength, but we have to believe, cut and hew, and build.

We can get too busy. I was doing a good and necessary thing, but I didn't stop a few moments and I missed the first rainbow. There are a lot of rainbows, but only one first rainbow, and I have learned to live, take advantage of, and enjoy each moment, because they do not return.

I learned to be grateful. Instead of complaining about getting off the mountain, I should have been on my knees thanking God that I was on a mountain".

The rest of Shem's message was broken from the stone and has not been found.

Whether these scraps of wood and this stone are faked, forged, or fantasy, you decide, but in any case, Shem does have a message that is still pertinent for us today.

Sinai

On the northern coast of Egypt, lies the city of Alexandria. The modern city sits atop the ruins of an ancient city that once was a center of knowledge of the known world. It once contained a vast library and it was here that Jewish scholars translated Hebrew Scriptures into Greek, the universal language of culture at that time. During some recent excavations, a sealed jar was unearthed which contained some scrolls written in ancient Hebrew, describing some of the wanderings of the Israelites in their journey to the Promised Land. While interesting, nothing new was unfolded, until a piece of parchment was discovered wrapped in the papyrus scrolls. This parchment contained sort of a journal of Aaron, the brother of Moses. The following are portions of that journal.

Red Sea crossing plus 135 days- sometimes I wonder how I got such a terrible job. I was supposed to be just a spokesman, but now I am supposed to control this surly multitude. They complained while we were in Egypt about their mistreatment and when God gave them the opportunity to be free, they were glad to do as He commanded. But in these few months, they seem to have forgotten. They forget how bad it was, they forget God's compassion, and they forget His display of power. Here we are at the foot of Sinai and these people are almost out of control. They seem to listen to what Moses has me tell them as long as he is here, but he has been gone over a month and they are getting very restless.

Red Sea crossing plus 140 days- I thought that when I got called up on the mountain with Moses, I would get enough respect that these people would listen and follow instructions, but they are getting out of hand. They seem to still have the same slave mentality that they had in Egypt and seem to be unable to think for themselves. They had watched their Egyptian taskmasters as they appeased their gods and noted their success and accomplishments, and cannot seem to grasp the concept of a loving God that just wants worship and obedience. The idea of an unseen God, no matter how He demonstrated His power, seems beyond their ability to grasp. They grow more restless by the hour, and something will soon have to be done. Maybe a good night's sleep will calm them down, or maybe Moses will come down before morning.

Red Sea crossing plus 141 days- Moses did not come down during the night and a night's sleep didn't help. I am going to talk to the loudest and see what it will take to quiet them down.

Red Sea crossing plus 142 days- it is almost midday and everyone that I have talked to is frightened and wants some visible object to worship. They want to think they have been freed and they believe that their freedom should allow them to have a celebration similar to those their former masters seemed to enjoy. Maybe we should compromise just a little.

Red Sea crossing plus 143 days - I have suggested we collect some gold earrings and make a small statue and then sing and dance and have a small party. It would relieve the tension a bit and everyone seemed to be in agreement.

Red Sea crossing plus 144 days- the party did get out of hand a little. The people seemed to forget who it was that led them out of Egypt and wanted to give credit to that silly little gold bull. That was bad enough, but then Moses came down from the mountain and saw all the celebration. I never saw him so angry. He took those stone tablets and broke them and smashed the gold statue. Worst of all, he blamed me. I tried to explain that it wasn't my fault. I was only doing something to pacify the people. I didn't think that little gold calf would replace God, but rather, just be an addition that they could see. I felt that these people needed a little fun for a change and a little party wouldn't hurt. The laws that God had sent down seemed a little strict and considering the circumstances and times, what we were doing wasn't that bad. Moses didn't agree and God did punish us.

This is all that was found of Aaron's manuscript. The rest of the story can be found in the Scriptures. God's commandments were only a little over a month old when His chosen people openly disobeyed and history records countless other times when they were disobeyed and the tragic consequences that have resulted.

Moses came down that mountain with stone tablet inscribed by God Himself. Those tablets were stone, thereby indicating they could not be altered or erased and would last forever. When the people disobeyed, those laws were not re-examined to determine if they were viable and the people never had a chance to vote on any of the laws. Those commandments were not authored to fit society, but rather society was to conform to them. For their disobedience, God was very angry and His chosen people were severely punished, and those commandments have never been repealed.

Aaron has a message for all ages, because over the centuries, mankind has not changed that much. We still are prone to compromise our beliefs at times, we still have troubles with all sorts of lesser gods, we offer the excuse that times have changed, and we still confuse fun with true happiness. The question is; how often would we give reason for Moses to get angry and smash those tablets?

A Small Mountain Near the Sea of Galilee

In 1947, a shepherd boy discovered some scrolls in a cave near the northwest shore of the Dead Sea, and he sold some of them for next to nothing because he didn't realize their value. Archeologists eventually heard about them and collected over 400 pieces of them and determined they were writings of a sect called the Essenes. The Essenes were even stricter in their interpretation of Scriptures and law than the Pharisees. So strict were they that they, for the most part, isolated themselves in sort of a commune to keep their religion pure. These writings are among the oldest ever discovered and have helped in understanding life and the beliefs at the time of Christ.

Although over 400 of these scrolls were found, preserved and studied, one of the scrolls the shepherd boy found and sold, recently surfaced at an antique store. It appears to be a report presented to the others about an ex-carpenter that was getting some fame and a large following. The reporter is nameless, but this is a report on what he had witnessed.

"I am an Essene and I was sent north and across the Jordan by my superiors to listen to a teacher who was drawing very large crowds. I was to report on what He had to say and to determine if His teachings would enhance our beliefs or were a threat to us. We are a very small minority and we are concerned that some might be lured away by His popularity. We believe that God's laws must be strictly adhered to and even the Pharisees take too many liberties with it. The views on the law by this teacher were of prime concern".

"I caught up with this teacher on a small mountain where He was addressing a large crowd and pushed my way into easy hearing distance. A large portion of the crowd stood farther away and was merely curious. They had heard of some miraculous healings and wanted to witness such an event. In the center of the crowd, were some very average people who listened intently and were looking for some deeper meaning and purpose to life as though their religion lacked the instructions for everyday living. They seemed to want a religion that would address their personal happiness and well being, define their role in society, and put some purpose and meaning into their rites and rituals.   Closest to Him were the weak, sick, and crippled, hoping for a miracle that would allow them to be productive and pain free. Mixed throughout the crowd were people like me, some just curious, some concerned with His effect on traditional beliefs, and a few prepared to "heckle".

"Within the next few hours, all would get what they came for. I, and those on the edge of the crowd would be amazed at the power he displayed as He did heal those who surrounded Him. No one could doubt that such power had to come from God, Himself. The healing did not come from a potion that would cure in days or months, but rather, it came instantly in the presence of the multitude. No one was excluded. There was not a disease too severe, a handicap too crippling, or any malady that He did not instantly cure, and He asked nothing in return. This man had to be sent by God.

"I was affected more by the words He spoke. He was concerned about the happiness of His followers. This is most unusual, because most religions, and I must confess, we Essenes too, are more concerned with appeasement and judgement than happiness of the people. It was most interesting as to what He suggested would make people happy. He did not mention wealth, power, celebration, or sensuality, but rather, meekness, humility, purity, honesty, and kindness. I could not disagree. The conventional pursuit of happiness does fail and our attempt to escape this pursuit by isolation also fails. Possibly, He is correct. We might also be looking in the wrong places and pursuing the wrong goals. I was impressed that He considered happiness as a most important part of religion".

"He also addressed the importance of the law. This was what I was most interested in. I was pleased to hear that He did not want to change the law, only to explain it. I thought we had done a pretty good job of explaining it. We had written all sorts of definitions as to what it meant and how it was to be applied, but He explained that how we viewed the law was of more importance. He said that sin comes from intent as much as from the deed, that we should worship because of awe and love rather than fear and that hatred and murder are virtually the same sin".

"He said that our praying, giving, and charity is a private matter between us and God. All this goes contrary to what I have been taught, but I see His point. Our concern has been defining and punishment, His approach is prevention by purifying thoughts and intent. He seemed to base His approach to life on love. His picture of

God is a loving and caring deity rather than one to be feared, and His solution to our daily problems is simply to love one another. The prophets of old often talked this way, but the world seems to prefer a harsher approach. The logic is sound, a world motivated by love would be ideal, but where does it start? His answer seems to be that it must start with each one of us and that by our words and deeds, the world would sit up and take notice".

"I must submit this report. I can find no fault with what I have heard. I must confess that His idealism should work. It would make the world a better place in which to live if everyone practiced it, but I feel that the little bit that I could do as just one person would have no impact. I would be a laughing stock and victimized rather than make a contribution to society. The power I witnessed, the concept of happiness, the beautiful interpretations of the law, and the idea of love as the basis of our relationships, puts my life in a new perspective. I must return to the commune and maybe I can share what I witnessed and make my little corner of the world a little brighter".

This is all we will ever hear of this Essene who had the privilege of witnessing Christ's "Sermon on the Mount". Herein lies the solution for all of the world's problems and so much of it goes unheeded. Who could ever dispute that if life, as outlined in this sermon, were practiced by the world's citizens would be happier, the world safer, and it would be a more enjoyable place to live?

We, like the Essene, too often return to our own little commune rather than spread the teaching of the "Itinerate Carpenter form Galilee".

Golgotha

On April 12,1961, Yuri Gargarin orbited the earth. He was a Russian astronaut and the first man in space. One of the comments he is reported as saying was; "I didn't see any angels out there". Of course, such a comment would be expected from a representative from an atheistic society. Some years later, the Russians orbited the Mir space station, operated it for a while, abandoned it, and then returned to conduct some further experiments. One of the astronauts seemed to mysteriously disappear after his successful return to earth and nothing more was heard of him.

Some time ago, a middle aged Russian returned to his family and friends after a very long assignment in Siberia. He had been assigned to an isolated weather station to monitor weather signals from weather satellites, and finally, as the Cold War ended, was allowed to go home. He tells this very interesting story.

"I was on a solitary mission and I was the first astronaut to re-enter the Mir space station and what I experienced and saw, caused me great concern. When I returned to earth and was debriefed, my report was hidden and I was assigned to Siberia so my story would not be heard. Today, there is a certain openness that allows me to share this story".

"I had studied and trained hard, was indoctrinated in Communism, and was selected for this special mission. I felt honored. I still recall the thrill of the blast-off and the excitement of discovery. We docked smoothly with the station and I was anxious to shed my space suit and experience the weightlessness and freedom of life in the station. As I was making myself comfortable, there appeared a figure, rather relaxed, and giving the impression that he had been waiting for me. I, at first, thought there must have been some sort of mistake, until he assured me that no one erred and this encounter was just between him and me. He said that he was an angel. My atheistic belief didn't include angels, but there was no way any other personality could be there. My engineering education excluded any other possibility, so I had no alternative but to believe him. He said to go about my work as if nothing had happened. This was good advice, since no one would believe me anyway, but to believe that I could go on as if nothing unusual was happening was asking a lot. Over the next few days, he proved to be an interesting companion and entertained me with some very interesting tales".

As he told his tales. I got the impression that he was sort of an eccentric angel, if angels can be eccentric. He said that the reason for his being in the space station was to show my comrades, and especially that Gargarin guy, that there were such things as angels. He said that the rest of the heavenly host wasn't bothered by some atheist boasting that he didn't see any angels, but he was, and he was going to make a point. He was making his point with me, but I could probably never share the experience without great jeopardy to my life. His very existence was enough to change my concept of life and its purpose and values, but one of his stories has changed my life forever and I feel I must share it.

About 2000 years ago, my angel friend was observing with great pride the interest that many people were showing in the teachings of Jesus Christ. This Son of God had been sent with a very special message and the local people were listening. They seemed impressed with His power and enthralled with His message of love. His fame had spread and soon His journeys took Him to Jerusalem, the very heart of the religious community, and even here, He attracted a large crowd. My angel friend thought that the message was finally being accepted and the leaders would welcome Him until he noted the jealousy of those who were supposed to be the religious leaders of the day. Here were the educated religious leaders, who had heard the law from childhood, studied the Scriptures extensively, and even taught what they had learned to others, plotting the downfall of the Son of God. This was insane! The most sacred portion of the law, the Ten Commandments, specifically dealt with murder and jealousy, and the ones who knew the law best were guilty of these thoughts. What could have founded these thoughts? Jesus Christ had done nothing to undermine the concept of a sovereign God. He had done nothing to change the instructions of man's responsibility to one another, and nothing He said or did would have an adverse effect on society. Of course, He did claim to be God's son, but the power He displayed should have proven that, even though He didn't defeat the mighty Roman Empire and once again establish a mighty nation as they had expected their Messiah to do. He did accuse them of unfair dealings in the name of religion and that did make them angry. They were wrong and they knew it.

The angel couldn't understand. Here were intelligent, educated, and religious people, capable of rational thought, who had allowed the sins of hatred and jealousy to blind them to what should have been some obvious truths. The angel was getting angry and getting angry was not angelic behavior. He watched through a mock trial, heard the sentence of death imposed, and witnessed the cruelty of the scourging.

The angel then became a little apologetic. He conceded that his actions should always be angelic, but when he saw what happened on that hill called Golgotha, he reacted and tore the curtain of the great Temple, the one that separated the worshippers from the most holy place, almost to the bottom. The angel conceded that the un-angelic display of temper that brought him into the space station was very mild compared to the one he displayed when he tore the curtain, but you never know how an eccentric angel will react.

The Russian astronaut acknowledged that the angel had reason to become angry and he had searched his soul and realized that he and his actions, and much of what happens all over the world, were enough to arouse the ire of an angel. Then he finished his story.

The angel was fearful that God might punish him for his temper tantrum, after all, it was not angelic and God did summons him to His very presence. The angel was fearful and knew that he had done wrong and expected a strong reprimand. Instead, God smiled and told him to go guard the tomb and tell those who might come that Christ had risen. God made it very clear that such an assignment was not a reward, but rather an act of forgiveness. In fact, the whole drama that took place on that hill was such a display of love and forgiveness that even angels couldn't understand.

The Last Hill

The last hill is an unnamed hill in Galilee, where Jesus told His eleven remaining disciples to meet Him, and where He said farewell and disappeared into the heavens. According to Matthew, they all worshipped Him, even though some still had some doubts. His last instructions to them were to spread the "Good News" all over the world. This commission is still binding. We have visited four other mountains and hills and you may not completely believe everything related about them but this last hill should also be our story.

I have that little hill on my farm, but I also have a much higher hill. From this higher hill, I can view much of the world around me. I can see the beauty in the distant valleys, but I can also see the junkyards, the landfills and the slums. While I can not help but to admire the beauty, I also must feel a responsibility to clean up the ugly. This ugly does not change by my sitting on this mountain, but rather by my climbing down and getting my hands dirty. I understand that I cannot clean up all the junk I see, but if I clean up a little and every one else cleans up a little, the job can be done, and I must also make sure that I don't add to the mess.

From the top of the mountain, I must realize that the entire world can see me. I make an easy target for all kinds of criticism and I will be judged by all who see me. When I am on this mountain, whether I am admiring the beauty or observing the mess, I am vulnerable to the opinions of everyone in the valley, therefore, I must be honest and present a good image.

Each of us, at times, sits on a hill or maybe even a mountain. None of us dare forever hide in a valley. Some people's hills are very small and some folks climb a pretty high mountain, but the road in this adventure we call life does have some hills. If we get high enough to see beauty, we are high enough to see the landfill, so if we are to enjoy the view, we have a responsibility to improve that view for others.

Each of us has many opportunities to write a story about spreading the "Good News". Our stories will all be different, as each will reflect our different talents and different opportunities. There are, however, some ways that are common to all of us that we should consider.

Remember Shem? He was worried about getting down that mountain. One of the best ways to spread the "Good News" is by optimism. This is not always easy and does not come without effort. It starts with a faith in the future. By now, all of us should know that all dry spells have ended, all rainy days have been followed by sunshine, spring has always came, and good fortune has always followed bad. We should have noticed that for the most part, we take life too seriously. We worry about things of a temporary nature or have no eternal values, and even worry about a lot of things that never even happen. Christianity is optimism at its best. It is based on faith. The very core of our belief is that God loves us and will take care of us. We believe that life is eternal and our short adventure on earth will be followed by endless happiness. We must also believe that happiness is more dependent on how we view a situation than the situation itself, and understand that our values must be placed in a proper perspective.

Remember Aaron? He compromised a little and made a golden calf. How many golden calves do we have? There is probably no better way to spread the "Good News" than through our views on earthly possessions. Their priorities in our lives, the way we acquire them, our work ethic, our stewardship, and our generosity, or lack of it, can speak so loud that any words we may utter are drowned out. Here we are most visible and the world wants to judge us by its standard. This phase of life is made more difficult as there are no universal or ironclad laws. Instead, it is a personal matter governed by rules which were spelled out when Christ explained stewardship and when He said that we must "do unto others as we would have them do unto us".

Remember the Essene? He was interested in the law and found that God's laws remain. When this world was created, the laws that were necessary for it to run smoothly and for the people to live together were created with it. They are timeless, and moral anarchy is disastrous, but man is ingenious in finding ways to circumvent them. As we present the "Good News", we must always be mindful that we are not to judge, and here we walk a very fine line. It is hard to hate the sin, but love the sinner, it is hard to be a friend and neighbor to those who view morality differently, it is hard to be moral and not appear self-righteous, and it is tempting to preach "do as I say, not as I do".

We do have the responsibility to represent the law. It must be the guideline for our daily life, and it is the only guideline for a happy, healthy, and safe society. We will all be judged by the law, not so much by our failures in obedience as our lack of effort, contempt, or compromise. For three years, Jesus traveled and taught, and His theme was an understanding of this law, now it is up to us.

Remember the eccentric angel? He couldn't completely comprehend the gift of forgiveness. This should be a most marketable commodity, except for one thing; we find it difficult to acknowledge our sins. We have a standard and ideal to which we must aspire, and although we try, and without exception, we fall short and then, so often, rather than ask forgiveness, we offer excuses. We like blanket coverage instead of looking for a specific sin and taking measures to eliminate that sin in the future. We can get comfortable with our weaknesses.

We also find it hard to comprehend forgiveness because we don't fully understand love. Our incomplete love as mortals makes it hard to forgive others and we fail to consider that God's perfect love results in complete forgiveness. Maybe a little practice by us would help us understand God a little better and help us to proclaim it to a skeptical world.

As practicing Christians, we should have many interesting mountain stories as we try to spread Christ's message. Sometimes we tell these stories well, sometimes we don't even realize we are telling a story, and sometimes we tell it very poorly. On occasions, we have a receptive audience, sometimes the noise of everyday life drowns out what we have to say, and sometimes we are even told to shut up, but from that mountain in Galilee, the message is still to spread it to the whole world.

The Message of Jesus Christ

He was born in an obscure village. He worked in a carpenter shop until He was thirty. He then became an itinerant preacher. He never held an office. He never had a family or owned a house. He didn't go to college. He had no credentials except Himself. He was only 33 when the public turned against Him. His friends ran away. He was turned over to His enemies and went through the mockery of a trial. He was nailed to a cross between two thieves. While He was dying, His executioners gambled for His clothing, the only property He had on earth. He was laid in a borrowed grave.

Nineteen centuries have come and gone and today He is the central figure of the human race. All the armies that ever marched, all the navies that ever sailed, all the parliaments that ever sat and all the kings that ever reigned have not affected the lives of people on this earth as much as that one solitary life.

Author Unknown

With such credentials, it is necessary to consider Jesus Christ. All great religions recognize Him and there are very few people who would be so bold to find fault with any of His teachings. No one has ever doubted the world would be a better place to live if His lessons of peaceful living and brotherly love were followed and the peace and serenity of those who use His teachings give them credibility. In spite of this credibility and in spite of the fact that His teachings are rarely disputed, an in depth study into these teachings is too seldom made. Even most religious instructions overlook much of what He was trying to explain and dwell on emotional or social issues, or assorted bits of scripture.

The scriptures are very brief, but five encounters with five different sorts of people can give a pretty good idea of His message to humanity if we only look closely. It should be noted that these encounters are not with the clergy or scholars, but with common people and often disliked people. His messages did not deal with religious or church law or ritual, but rather with the everyday life of everyday people.

My request is that you read these stories very carefully and look for the message He was trying to convey, and then imagine a world that followed His advice. My concept of Jesus is not of a preacher, but rather a teacher. He did not play on emotion, but rather taught by examples that could be easily understood. While these encounters happened two thousand years ago, they are still pertinent today inasmuch as the problems addressed are still with us, and it is not because His solutions will not work, but rather they just get ignored. Please remember that Jesus only taught for three years and these teachings are seldom disputed by any religion. Only His last three days define a religion. While His blueprint for eternity seems not to appeal to a lot of people, His solutions for a peaceful and happy society should be studied and practiced by all.

The Roman Officer

This story is recorded in the Scriptures in Matthew 8; 5-13 and to understand this story, you have to understand the times. The entire known world was ruled by Rome and in this area, the Romans considered the Jews as quite a problem. They were viewed as potential troublemakers because of their religious beliefs which included watching for a Messiah who would restore their former nation, in fact, a Jewish uprising about 200 years previously, led to the Roman acquisition of this area. Of course, they knew of this history and didn't want that kind of trouble. They were worried when a man named John amassed quite a following in the wilderness east of the Jordan River by proclaiming that the Messiah was at hand and the Roman government was not about to take any chances of an insurrection, so they arrested him and imprisoned him. A garrison of soldiers was stationed at the nearby town of Capernaum and was on the alert for any signs of trouble. No doubt, they were to make their presence obvious. The Roman government prided itself in being firm but fair and its authority was not questioned and seldom tested.

At the time of this story, Jesus had been teaching in the synagogue in his hometown of Nazareth. The folks in His hometown were a little angry that He had performed some miracles away from home and had not cured everyone in His hometown first, so they asked Him to leave. He went a few miles south to the town of Capernaum. Along the way, He had picked up a few disciples, cured some sick people, and stated His message of love and purity. This message became very popular and the fame of Jesus spread very quickly.

One of those hearing of Jesus was a Roman officer and he went looking for Him. This seemed like a lot of trouble. Any appearance of a Roman officer could only mean trouble. The army was not exactly welcome in Capernaum and when an officer came looking for someone, especially someone who was attracting a lot of attention, it was real cause for alarm. Officers were not scholars looking for a bit of wisdom, but rather fighting men sent to forcibly, if necessary, preserve the peace. These were men trained to kill in hand to hand combat, and one of such rank had probably proven himself and had probably ordered his men to kill also. Such a person would be reason for panic. But this time, the officer wanted help.

The officer had a slave boy who was partially paralyzed and in great pain, and we can only guess whether it was out of compassion or probable loss of a valuable piece of property, but the officer came to Jesus for help. He wanted Jesus to heal this sick boy and Jesus consented to go to his home and heal the boy.

Then the officer expressed the thought that he, a man of violence, was not worthy to have a man who was teaching peace and love to come into his home, but that Jesus could do the healing by just saying "Be healed." The officer understood authority. He knew he had to obey orders from Rome and that he could order his men even to their death and from what he had heard, Jesus had the authority to tell that illness to leave and it would go. Jesus was impressed, healed the boy, and pointed out to the crowd around, the faith the officer had in His authority and the necessity of such a faith.

That Roman officer understood something that is often hard to understand, especially in a culture that takes great pride in its freedom and so often fails to submit to authority. In the quest for that priceless freedom, it is easy to prefer anarchy to authority.

Our culture seems to encourage it early in life, when small children show no respect for elders, teachers, or even their parents. One of our major educational problems is discipline, even at the college level. The laws of our land and even the laws of God seem to be only obeyed if convenient or breaking them cannot be rationalized. Our full jails attest to our problems with accepting authority.

Just as dangerous, is submitting to the wrong authority. There are many sects and creeds that play on emotion, or are based on tiny segments of Scripture or some ancient or mystic religion, or are the invention of some charismatic person. There are those who believe their senses are their masters and if it feels good, do it. Also there are those who believe that civil law is all the authority they need and to be law abiding citizens is all the authority they need.

The lesson we should learn from the encounter with the Roman officer. Is that we are under God's authority. Unless we accept God as our Creator, our world is only a happening of coincidence and chance. Unless we accept the Scriptures as the word of God, any pamphlet by any author should be acceptable for our behavior. Unless we accept the commandments as God's law, we may as well make up our own and change it whenever convenient. Unless we acknowledge that God has the authority to judge, we can allow the whims of society to determine our conduct.

What do you suppose would have happened if Jesus had refused to cure that sick slave boy, after all, the Roman officer was a pagan and an enemy of the local people? What do you suppose would have happened if Jesus didn't have the power to heal the boy and he would have died? The message of this story is loud and clear. Not only did Jesus have the power to heal, but He even had the authority and compassion to heal a hated Roman.

Our faith must be based on those two things. Our salvation is at the discretion of God and paid for by that "Amazing Grace" and no matter how nice we are, we can not earn or purchase salvation. It is important that we recognize God's authority as well as that Roman soldier did.

A Woman at a Well

This story is recorded in John 4; 4-45 and is a story of an interesting woman who was a very unusual person and a very unlikely teacher of an important lesson. She was a resident of the small village of Sychar in the province of Samaria. Sychar was a small town, maybe a couple hundred residents; at least John called it a village. It was located along a busy road that led from Judea to Galilee, but was usually bypassed by good Jews because it was in hated Samaria. Of great importance to the town was a well that had been dug on land once owned by their ancestor, Jacob. This well provided water for the town and for travelers along the road.

Jesus and His disciples were travelling north from Judea to Galilee. Unlike most Jews, Jesus went through Samaria because it was the shortest route and Jesus never lost the opportunity to point out that the prejudice against the Samaritans was silly. The Jews regarded the Samaritans as a sort of half-breed race. They both had Abraham as a common ancestor, but were not exiled to Babylon as the Judeans were. They had also intermarried with people from other nations. They also did not recognize the temple in Jerusalem as their center of worship, but rather Mount Gerizam, and therefore had done nothing to fund and rebuild the temple. For these reasons, good Jews considered them as pagans, but Jesus, on many occasions, made reference to them to teach lessons on tolerance and love.

The trip from Judea to Galilee was about seventy miles, a short trip, unless you had to walk. Sychar was about thirty miles into the journey. Twenty miles was considered a day's travel for a family on a pilgrimage, so possibly, this was about noon on the second day. At least, it was hot, and Jesus and his followers were taking a break. They wanted a bite to eat and something to drink. There was probably no place in town that served meals, at least the disciples went into the town to find something to eat. They probably knocked on some doors until they found someone who had an extra loaf of bread or some fruit. It was probably no small task to find food for a dozen people in that small town. While the disciples were looking for food, Jesus waited by the well for someone with a rope and bucket to get them a drink.

While Jesus was waiting, this woman showed up and she was quite a woman. She was probably rather young, very pretty, smart, outgoing and not at all bashful. Walking across town to get water was usually done in the cool of the day, but for some reason she had run out of water. She probably had an earthen water pot, which she balanced on her head. She mentioned that it was a long walk, in even a small town, it could easily have been a mile round trip. Her water pot could have weighed ten pounds, probably held three gallons of water, which meant she had to carry about thirty -five pounds on her head all the way across town. Such a task insured that she had good posture, was quite strong, and in good shape. Jesus asked her for a drink and she recognized him as a Galilean and mentioned that it was very unusual for a Jew to speak to a Samaritan, especially a woman. Jesus replied that instead of him asking her for just a drink, she should be asking him for living water. She laughed at him because he didn't even have a rope to get any kind of water, but liked the notion of not having to carry a heavy jar of water all the way across town every day. Jesus told her to go get her husband and he would explain what he meant.

She said that she didn't have a husband and Jesus surprised her by telling her that she had had five husbands and was not married to the person with whom she was now living. You can be sure such a woman would be well known all over that small town. She must have been quite a beauty to attract six of the eligible young men in a small town and must have had a sort of independent nature to have dumped or have been dumped by five of them. In any event, you can be sure everyone in town knew who she was.

When Jesus told her of her personal life, she recognized that he was not just an ordinary traveler. She thought that he must have been some sort of prophet, and asked him where was the proper place to worship. She evidently knew of the traditions and the resulting conflicts between the Samaritans and the Jews and tried to put Jesus on the spot. The answer he gave is most important. Jesus said that the place was not important, but that how we worshipped was, and that inasmuch as God is a spirit, we must worship Him in Spirit and in truth.

The dictionary defines worship as the act of paying reverence to God. This poses the question of how good we are at worshipping. Although they can be helpful, ritual, attendance, holding office or even generous giving is not necessarily worship. Worship does not always happen in churches, nor should it. Worship need not be shouting, dancing, or arm waving, nor need it be somber or accented with tears. Worship is a state of mind. Worship is not something that happens to you, but rather something that you consciously do. Worship requires effort and God requires worship.

The basis of worship is recognizing, appreciating, and enjoying God's marvelous creation. All too often we take for granted the world around us and fail to see beauty, fail to marvel at its precision, and ignore God's hand in the plan of our world. We fail to enjoy the differences of those around us, and ignore the similarities that make us brothers. We cry to God in our sorrow and forget Him in our happy times. We expect God to come to us and fail to go to Him. We covet His love and forget that we must try to make ourselves loveable.

Worship also requires humility and as a rule, most of us are not very humble. We are taught equality and sometimes believe that includes equality with God. We take all the credit for our successes, rely too much on our knowledge and all the gadgets which it has produced, and somehow get the notion that being nice is the key to heaven rather than that "Amazing Grace".

Jesus used this woman to teach a very valuable lesson even though she was an unlikely messenger. She was a Samaritan, a sinner, and no scholar, but she was effective. The whole town came to listen to Jesus and instead of just passing through, He stayed two days and the people listened. From that encounter comes an important message for us today.

God does require us to worship Him. A church can provide an atmosphere for worship, but the act of worship is a personal effort. Worship is not entertainment, an excellent sermon, a good choir, or even generous giving. Mount Gerizam or the temple in Jerusalem was not the issue, but rather a condition of honesty and sincerity.

A Poor Widow

Matthew records this story in the 12th chapter and verses 41 to 44 and Luke tells it in chapter 21 and verses 1 to 4. The event occurred near the end of Jesus' ministry. Jesus had been teaching for about three years and became quite famous in that corner of the world. The area of most of his teachings was in Galilee, a quiet agricultural area, and the people listened to what He had to say. But there came a time when He had to move on.

His message was pretty well received in the quiet countryside, but when He went to the religious, political, and cultural center in Jerusalem, His reception was much different. His fame had preceded

Him, and the common folk had welcomed Him into Jerusalem with a "palm leaf parade", but those educated in religion waited for him and tried to embarrass Him with questions about Jewish law. This was "home court" for those religious leaders and they were anxious to get their hands on that carpenter from Galilee.

Jesus had gone to the Temple and noted that many wealthy people were giving openly and generously, but a poor widow was putting just a few cents into the collection box. Jesus noticed this and pointed out that the widow's tiny gift was greater in the eyes of God than the large gifts of the wealthy.

Sometimes this is hard to understand. Everyone knows that there is much need for charity in our world. We know that churches need a lot of money to operate and for their outreaches. There are all sorts of requests for money for medical research that only can come from private sources. There are the homeless, abused, and others that society must care for. And there are those in foreign lands where opportunity is very limited and all sorts of help is needed. An offering of just a couple pennies can support none of this. It is evident that the contributions of the more affluent are quite necessary.

The point that Jesus was trying to make was that all of us need to share what we have, no matter how small. The true value in giving is not only in what the money accomplishes but also what it tells about our appreciation for what we have. Our charity should not only be an act of compassion but also an expression of thanks and recognition that we are stewards of this good earth. The rich folks who were giving of their wealth while the poor woman was giving in spite of her poverty might have been a bit proud of their large gifts. Maybe they wanted the world to note how nice they were and were in reality boasting of their wealth and trying to earn God's favor.

In Jesus' ministry, He mentioned wealth on many occasions. There was the rich young man wanted to be a follower, but wouldn't give up his wealth to do so. There were the people who asked about paying taxes and prompted the response of "giving to Caesar what is Caesar's and to God, what is God's". And there were the moneychangers in the Temple who were the objects of Jesus' wrath. All these encounters point out that there are certain obligations connected to our wealth, both in acquiring it and in using it, whether it is great or small.

In the discussion with His disciples following the departure of the young man, they asked; "If a very moral young man cannot get into heaven just because he has lots of money, who can"? The answer Jesus gave was; "All things are possible with God." It was here that Jesus is often quoted when He said that it is easier for a camel to go through an eye of a needle than a rich man to get into heaven.

This brings up the scary question of; "Am I rich"? And the answer is that most of us are extremely rich. Most of us have the choice of all the healthful and tasty food we need, and probably waste more than people in many lands can afford, and eating too much is more of a problem than not having enough to eat. We are well dressed, both for comfort and for style. Even a humble home today contains more luxuries than even a rich person could buy a couple generations ago. We can afford automobiles, medical attention, and all sorts of gadgets and toys. Most have good jobs, savings, pension plans, investments, and opportunities that make our lives comfortable. Unless there are very small camels, or very large needles, we all have a problem.

Jesus was trying to make three points in the encounters with people concerning wealth. The poor widow was praised because she sacrificed what could be called some necessities of life as an act of worship and appreciation. In His encounters with the moneychangers, He was stressing that money must be earned honestly. He was telling the rich people in the temple and the rich young man that giving money to the temple or the poor was not primarily to help the poor or maintain the Temple, but rather for their benefit. While all of us like to see the results of our charity, a proper concept of stewardship is for self-help. One of the poorest notions that so many religious institutions foster is that the reason for giving is to build buildings, help the unfortunate, or even to spread the gospel. Jesus tried to point out that giving should be an act of worship, an expression of thankfulness, and an acknowledgement of the bounty of God's world, and that it is for us to use that bounty wisely. When this concept is understood, there will be plenty of funds for beautiful buildings, the unfortunate will get plenty of help, and spreading the gospel will not be hindered by lack of funds.

Another point Jesus was trying to make was that any entry into Heaven could not be earned by the wealthy or denied because of poverty. Entry into heaven is only possible by God's love and forgiveness. We can't earn it and we can't buy it. We are all pretty nice, and few of us are hungry, homeless, or clothed in rags, and most of us can afford more than that poor widow, but we better not use our wealth to deal our way into heaven or a lack of it for not sharing. If we would be so bold as to try to deal, we would be walking instead of driving, putting a "for sale" sign on our homes, and cashing in our bonds and passing out the money to the homeless. Jesus is not asking us to give all we have to the poor, unless our wealth is our number one priority. He is asking that we understand that this is God's world and we are to share with those in need, not because they need it, but rather, because we need to acknowledge that we are but stewards of this good earth for a short time.

Feeding the 5000

This must be a very important story because it is recorded in all four Gospels. It is usually told as an encounter between Jesus and 5000 people, but as John tells the story, it is also an encounter between Jesus and a boy with a lunch.

John the Baptist had just been beheaded and Jesus was teaching in Galilee, and attracting a lot of attention. In fact Herod was quite concerned about the attention He was attracting and because of a guilty conscience and being a bit superstitious, even thought that John might have come back to life. The crowds were everywhere and Jesus and the disciples wanted to get away for a short break and a bite to eat, so they took a boat and crossed the north end of the sea into a sparsely settled area. The crowds wanted to hear more, so they went by land around the end of the sea. Matthew says that Jesus did get away for a little while, but Mark says that some of the crowd was already waiting when He arrived. In any event, Jesus attracted a very large crowd in a sparsely settled area.

All four Gospels state that the crowd was over 5000 people. John does mention that some of the crowd was families on a pilgrimage to Jerusalem to celebrate the Passover, but even so, it is difficult to imagine such a large crowd in an area of small villages. It is evident that most of the crowd was not local people.

The Gospels relate that late in the afternoon, the disciples grew concerned about the crowd getting hungry. They cited the fact that it would be difficult, if not impossible, to find food for so many people in that area and even if they could, the cost would be prohibitive. Each of these problems should be quite evident. Even in today's culture, it would take several McDonalds to handle 100 busloads of people even if they were given several days' notice. The disciples raise the question and Jesus told them to just do it. This was a seemingly impossible task because it is doubtful if there was enough food for sale in all the local villages for a fraction of that many people.

It must also be remembered that those in the crowd also knew of the situation. Those on the pilgrimage to Jerusalem would have packed enough provision for at least four days, at least that was the time usually allotted for such a trip and enough provisions were usually carried for the whole trip. It is also hard to believe that most of the local people would not have packed a lunch if they had intended to stay all day. Those were the days before "fast-food" and even grocery stores and people had to take this into consideration when they left home. It is also hard to believe that the boy with his bread and fish was the only one in that crowd properly prepared. There was probably enough food in that crowd to feed everybody. A miracle did occur, everybody ate, and there was even some left over.

Just what was that miracle? I have no doubt that Jesus could have produced food from some rocks, or from the dirt, or just out of thin air, but did He have to? If I was anxious to hear what this teacher had to say and had chased him into an area where there was nothing to eat I would have either packed a lunch or gone home and looked for him the next day. When it was time to eat, I would have gathered my family, went off to the side and eaten. The notion of sharing what I had would not have entered my mind until that itinerate teacher mentioned that it was suppertime and some little boy was willing to share his meager lunch. I believe that when that boy offered his lunch, I would have looked around to see if anyone nearby could use some of what I had, or just wanted to have company for supper. I believe the real miracle was people sharing.

The Gospel writers didn't say how Jesus did it. They didn't record whether the food magically appeared or whether it was people sharing what they had, but the fact that a kid was willing to share must have been important or it would have not been mentioned. This was not a rescue from starvation. Everyone would have survived if no food was available, but it changed a long service into a fellowship. John did say that the people were amazed and would even considered making him a king, but Jesus left and went into the hills alone.

No matter how you want to view this miracle, as a lot of food just appearing, or people sharing because a boy was willing to share, the important message for us is sharing. Stewardship is returning to God a part of what really is his, but sharing concerns a relationship between people. It also concerns more than wealth. It might be five loaves and two fish, it might be a little time, it might be a smile, it might be a helping hand, or it might be a hug or a shoulder to cry on. Everyone has something to share and everyone has at some time needed help from others.

In our age of affluence and materialism, a lesson in sharing is very important. Small children are probably taught to share their toys, but formal education seems to be based on getting instead of giving. Young people are told to stay in school or continue their education because of the extra income they can expect and the notion that they should be preparing themselves to be better persons or better citizens is rarely mentioned. It seems that when people do share, they like to "give at the office" or pay more in taxes and let governments do it, rather than getting their hands dirty by actually touching someone in need. We so often look at social problems as problems solved by money and overlook the value of a caring and helping hand.

We also tend to only share what is left over. That young boy was willing to go a bit hungry so that someone else could eat. His mother must have packed him a nice lunch, and that lunch was not packed with the idea that anyone else would need part of it.

Anyone would gladly share what he couldn't eat, but it might be a little different if he would still be a little hungry. People might be inclined to share if it was a matter of survival, but no one would have died if the boy had eaten all of his lunch. It was simply sharing the common little things of life to make other lives a little happier, and everyone has such opportunities almost every day.

The boy was also prepared to share. He had something to give. All of us can do the world a big favor if we also pack a lunch. We can be happy, optimistic, caring, generous, and assume our responsibilities. None of us will probably ever have the opportunity to feed a crowd of 5000, but we can feed 5000, one person at a time. We probably meet very few people who need food, but we probably meet a lot of people who need a kind word, a little encouragement, or a hug, and when we share with others, a little miracle always happens.

The Ten Lepers

This story was related by Dr. Luke in verses 11- 19 in the 17th chapter. Jesus had been teaching in Galilee and was heading south toward Jerusalem. He and the disciples were near the border between Galilee and Samaria when ten lepers approached them. Leprosy was a most dreaded disease and at time and to them, it was any disease that was evident by sores on the skin. Two chapters in the book of Leviticus are devoted to detecting and preventing its spread. This is interesting because the association between disease and contagion and a sort of quarantine to prevent the spread of disease was not a common practice at that time. Lepers were banished from homes and towns by religious law. Life for a leper became just a matter of survival.

The disease must have been quite a problem in this area, inasmuch as there was a colony of at least ten around this small town. There was no known cure and even very little relief from the pain from the disease was known. These men were doomed to die a very lonely and painful death.

Jesus had been teaching at times in that area and His fame had evidently reached those lonely lepers. They must have heard that He had healed some very sick people and even some lepers. They knew the law and so they kept their distance and shouted for Jesus to help them. Jesus also knew the law and told them to go to the Local Jewish priest and show him that they were healed, because they would still be considered lepers until the priest confirmed that the terrible sores were completely healed.

Just imagine the happiness of these ten people. They could return to their homes, to their wives, and their children. They could visit with their neighbors and return to work. They would look presentable and the pain would be gone. One came back and fell flat on the ground in front of Jesus and thanked God for the healing. Jesus then asked; "Where are the other nine"? He also noted that the one giving thanks was a Samaritan.

This is a familiar story and it is usually implied that those nine lepers were not thankful. It is easy to imagine how anxious these people were to get back home and get on with life. I find it hard to believe that not every one of them was not thankful, but I can also understand why only one immediately returned and expressed thanks. There is a lot of difference between being thankful and giving thanks and even a ratio of one in ten might be a little high most of the time.

Every one of us has many reasons to be thankful. We live at a time and in a place where freedom, peace and prosperity are taken for granted. We have plenty to eat, clothes for style and comfort, and all sorts of tools and gadgets to make our lives easy and enjoyable. None of us have leprosy. We have a holiday to remind us to be thankful and we hear from many sources to count our blessings. If any of those ten lepers were asked if he was thankful he was rid of the disease, he would have no doubt looked at the questioner and implied that he was crazy to ask such a question, and gladly told how thankful he was. Each one probably expressed to family and friends their thankfulness, but they forgot to say "thank you "to God. They were like a three-year-old that says "thank you" after being reminded. God expected a little more from these mature men.

He also expects the same from each of us. If any of us were asked, we could make a big list of our blessings, but then we might temper our thanks. We appreciate living in our great nation, but then we want to give credit to patriots, pioneers, or presidents. We are thankful for electric lights, running water, and telephones, but want to give credit to inventors, corporations, and our ability to pay the bill. We are thankful for nice homes, shining automobiles, and bank accounts, but then say we worked hard for it. We are glad we do not have leprosy, but give credit to good medical attention. So often, we are part of the nine.

We have so much more than any of that. We have been granted an existence in a marvelous and intricate world. We live in this world as a unique and special person created in the very likeness of God, Himself. We are a spiritual creation destined for an eternal existence outside our ability to understand. We have been granted the senses to make our brief stay on earth enjoyable. We can comprehend beauty, communicate with one another, and have the capacity to love. We are social by nature and we can share with family and friends our adventures, problems and rewards.

We have even been given instructions in how to make our stay on earth happy and rewarding. There are only ten rules and they seem simple, but life is a complicated adventure and we all find ourselves making poor judgements and mistakes. Here, we must be especially thankful, because of His great love for us, God has devised a plan for our atonement, and if we accept, we will be rewarded with eternal life. The truth is that we have a better deal than those lepers. Their reward was for a brief lifetime, ours is eternal. It would seem only appropriate that we joined that Samaritan leper and expressed our thanks. Those other nine did what would be considered a good thing. They hurried to their families and jobs and became productive citizens again, but that Samaritan did a better thing, and it only took a moment, he said "thank you". It might be well to check our line of communication with God. Is it 911 or "thank you"?

Charlie Cole

My Conclusion

I find what we call life is a very interesting and wonderful adventure. This journey is within a world of beauty, vastness, mystery and precision, and concerns challenge, fellowship and change. My close contact with the soil has inspired me to enjoy and compelled me to appreciate, and therefore share, part of this wonderful journey.

I enjoy this world of beauty. I can find it in green grass and growing crops. I can see color in blue skies, green trees, and flowers. I see it in innocent faces of children, smiling faces of happy adults, and in deeds of kindness and sharing. But I have also discovered that you have to look for it and be able to recognize it when you see it.

I see a vast creation when I see the stars or travel across plains or view a mountain. I have looked down from mountain tops, have looked at the endless sea, and have read of our attempts to explore the universe, and am in awe of the Creator of all of this. But in a time when speed and distance seem to make our world much smaller, I have also been able to find enjoyment in walking through fields and forests and looking for little details that speed passes over. A mile is a very short distance on an interstate highway, but is a long walk and can be filled with many surprises of a vast miniature world when examined closely and taken at leisure pace.

There is a certain mystery in this world that adds to the excitement. There are things and situations that can not be explained by science or logic, and hopefully, there will always be things that remain a mystery. There are the migrating birds, the intricate design of a honeycomb, and the many other instincts that allows wildlife to survive. There is the mystery of who teaches a spider how to spin a web, who taught the oriole to weave a nest, or how a barn swallow discovered that a little mud could be fashioned into a safe place to raise the next generation. Such mysteries should keep us humble.

I recognize precision and depend on this precision for the seasons to change, or as I use the laws of physics or mathematics in work or play. I know that I can depend on these laws and that they are a common denominator between all others and me. I know that the laws of mathematics and science that I learned in school many years ago are the same as are learned by my grandchildren, and I marvel at the use that has been made of these laws as I use today's technology. While at the moment it may not seem to be a blessing, repairing the tools necessary to till the good earth has given me an understanding of mechanics and also an appreciation of the tools and toys we too often just take for granted. Why and how these tools and toys work, and even how they are made, cause me to appreciate the precision of our world.

I welcome challenge and enjoy the feeling of accomplishment and the satisfaction of a job well done, and even understand the necessity of lessons that only failure seems to be able to teach. I have learned that for any happiness, there must be some aims and goals. These goals must also be unattainable, or at least projected to greater heights as they are reached. This is especially true of our morality. No one is ever so good that he needs no improvement, and if anyone so believes, his standards of morality are set much too low. As I experience this great adventure, I realize more than ever that the Creator knew what it would take for mankind to live happily and that His commandments were given for this purpose. I also understand that the only hope for peace and serenity on this earth is for us, the created, to live by "The Golden Rule". To comply with these lofty standards, should be our ultimate aim and they do set a standard to which we can only aspire.

I find the world to be full of a lot of interesting people. I have noted that each one is unique, yet there is a common thread that assures me that we are all brothers. I have found that there is good in all, and at least a bit of evil in all and each of us choose, moment by moment, which will prevail. I am encouraged when I hear of acts of kindness and mercy, and I find it hard to understand man's inhumanity to man, hatred of one another, wars, and violence. I firmly believe that God loves each of us and is more saddened than angered when we do not make ourselves loveable, and probably sheds a tear when one of His beloved must endure eternal punishment because of disobedience.

I also see a certain stupidity in mankind. In spite of his ability to invent, learn, and build, he fails to learn from history. He seems to be inclined to live for the moment with little thought for the future or learn from the lessons from the past or from watching others. Most of the heartaches we suffer are because we forget that the journey of life is a series of cause and effect. As I check out my failures, heartaches, and disappointments, most could have been prevented had I heeded this lesson. Impatience, believing "it just can't happen to me", forgetting past experiences or not learning from the experience of others, and "everybody else does it" are sure formulas for heartache. We also often fail to consider that a part of this great adventure includes pain and sadness and coping with adversity must be expected.

I also believe that we are tempted to take life too seriously, at least the wrong things in life. We are tempted to spend far too much time and expend far too much energy on the pursuit of temporary pleasure. We are afraid to laugh at ourselves and allow our feeling to get hurt too easily. This is really a funny world because it is inhabited by people doing funny things. While teasing can be cruel, I believe that there is an art to teasing that is underdeveloped and is necessary for happiness. I find that most people like to be teased if it is done in a spirit of mutual fun. Life does pose many serious situations, but most of these can be addressed and made easier when humor is used with discretion.

I see the world changing in many ways and very fast, and while all change is not good, change is necessary for progress and progress is a trait of civilized humanity. These changes, especially in communication, make the world smaller and move at a faster pace, and are very intrusive into private life. Personal responsibility, family values, and even national heritage seem to have suffered and are in need of special attention. Not only does the world change, but I also change, and some of this change is not welcome. As I age, I lose muscle tone and energy and gain a few aches and pains. Some of this change is very good. I gain new friends, add to my knowledge and experiences, and become aware of my spiritual being.

My connection with the good earth has convinced me that this world was created by an Intelligence with knowledge that humanity cannot begin to comprehend. Any notion of coincidence forming our wonderful world overlooks the countless details that are included in even the simplest plant or animal and the environment in which they live. My connection with the good earth has caused me to appreciate these countless details and to hold in awe their Creator as I see them all around me and utilize them in my daily life. Studies and experiments have discovered many of nature's secrets and ways to use these secrets, but discovering them is much different than creating them.

I note that there seems to be a universal quest for something we call happiness, and it often seems to be an elusive condition. Many have amassed great fortunes and not found happiness, many have attained great fame and not found it, and others have gained great knowledge and were still unhappy. Many have tried to cover unhappiness with "fun" and found this to fail. Abraham Lincoln said that people are about as happy as they want to be, and I must agree. Happiness comes from within and is attained when we live out lives as the Creator intended us to live.

Everyday I read the obituaries in the newspapers, and all to often read of people I knew. From this, I become more aware every day that my adventure on earth is limited. I also become aware that I will leave a heritage. It may be large or small, good or bad, and probably a little of both, but if I have lived rather than just existed, I will leave some mark. There will be no statues erected in my memory and memories of me will be short lived, but the greatest part of the challenge of this great adventure is for me to leave the world a little better than I found it. There is a debt owed to following generations, those around you, and to God for the privilege of this great adventure. Recognizing and paying this debt might bring eternal or historic rewards, but probably the greatest rewards will be realized along the way. There will be the love shared with a spouse, there will be the hugs from children, there will be the respect of friends and neighbors, and there will be a peace and serenity that only allegiance and obedience to God can bring. No life can be complete without a consideration of eternity. While this might be a dimension beyond our ability to begin to understand, few deny its existence. The same is true of our soul Somehow, the wonders I experience as I work with the good earth, not only establish the existence of both, but also make the eternal journey of my soul a matter of prime importance. If the wonderful adventure I am experiencing on this earth is an indication of my eternal journey, it will indeed be an exciting adventure.

I am sure many have enjoyed their adventure on earth as much as I, and have done so without a connection to the soil, but I feel blessed that in a world troubled with complicated problems, I have been able to find simple answers as I connect the soil to the adventure of my soul. It has been a pleasure to reminisce and to share some simple moments and the lessons I have learned from them, with the hope that they will also be of value to those who read them.

www.ingramcontent.com/pod-product-compliance
Lightning Source LLC
Chambersburg PA
CBHW051443280526
45785CB00003B/1412